Legwork

AN INSPIRING JOURNEY
THROUGH A CHRONIC ILLNESS

Ellen Burstein MacFarlane

WITH PATRICIA BURSTEIN

A LISA DREW BOOK

CHARLES SCRIBNER'S SONS

New York London Toronto Sydney Tokyo Singapore

CHARLES SCRIBNER'S SONS
Rockefeller Center
1230 Avenue of the Americas
New York, New York 10020

Manufactured in the United States of America

1   3   5   7   9   10   8   6   4   2

Library of Congress Catalog Card Number 94-67736

ISBN 0-02-578110-3

To my mother, Judge Beatrice S. Burstein, for her love and wisdom; to my sisters—Karen, for her affection and guidance; Patricia (my twin), who helped me resolve my past and open up my future; Jessica, for her sensitivity, laughter, and intelligence, and who shows me how to enjoy life; to my brothers— Johnny, for his warmth, great humor, and encouragement; and Judd, my friend and favorite attorney; and to my sister-in-law Chrissy and my delightful nephew Devin.

And for my late father, Herbert Burstein, who taught me about justice, truth, and never giving up.

It's all about love!

Contents

CONTENTS

Acknowledgments

My thanks to my editor, Lisa Drew, for her knowledge, support, and thoughtfulness at every turn; her assistant, Katherine Boyle, for her efficiency, thoroughness, and charm; and my literary agent, Elaine Markson, who believed in my story and made this book possible.

And to the National Multiple Sclerosis Society and its Central Florida chapter for their great dedication to helping those with MS.

Canine Companions for Independence for my treasured golden retriever, Butter, and the animals they raise to assist people like me.

My doctors Steven Rosenberg, Labe Scheinberg, and Herman Weinreb for their expertise and compassion.

My favorite aide and good friend, Bonita Stamper, and her husband, Bill, and their daughter, Charnita, who never object to the long hours she devotes to me.

Dr. Roy Douglas and the staff of the Los Angeles Medical Group for their help.

Brian MacFarlane, my former husband and now great friend, for his encouragement and guidance, and Tori and Amy MacFarlane, "my special girls."

Joanna Hall, Jacque Wishon, Sheelah Ryan, Marsha Temple, and Isaac Manor and his terrific children, Ben and Maytal, for their generosity and friendship.

Mike Schweitzer, president and general manager of WCPX-TV and one of the most decent human beings I've ever known; my pal R. C. Lee; my computer buddy Frank Torbert; Gloria Roberson for her dedication and support; Charna Wiese; and George Tyll.

And the many others who have made it possible for me to move on with my life, including Ron Parsons for his unfailing generosity; Cary Koplin; Dieter Hammerling; the staff of Sanlando Springs Animal Hospital, and Butter's veterinarian, Dr. Jim Brockman; Dr. Stuart Wasser; Larry Mosley; Gladys Alvarez; Myrna Moes; Clive Wagner; Katherine Sartor; and, as always, Vera Irving and James Speller.

Introduction

Legwork: An Inspiring Journey Through a Chronic Illness is the story of my life with multiple sclerosis, a disease of the central nervous system. But this is not just about me. It can happen to anyone. We are all only an illness or accident away from a wheelchair and a charlatan.

This is a true story about hope and defeat; promise and deception; falling down and getting up. Ultimately, it is legwork, my stock-in-trade as a television investigative consumer reporter, chasing and exposing crooks and swindlers who cheat people out of their most prized possessions and life savings, that enables me to stop the cruelest cheat of them all.

Yet, in spite of what became my worst defeat and most humiliating experience, I recover and make the journey back to myself. Despite the losses inflicted by MS, my spirit refuses to shut down, even as my body often does.

MS has taken away my mobility and stripped me of my independence. But it has not beaten me. Whenever it shoves me back, I find strength to go forward. Legwork, after all, is really about standing up—in or out of a wheelchair—for what is honorable and decent. It is a story that belongs to anyone, disabled, homeless, or disenfranchised, who is vulnerable.

My twin sister, Patricia, and I hope my story will inspire, inform, and make a difference in many lives.

So how do I begin? First, I tell the truth.

Part I

Between the idea
And the reality
Between the motion
And the act
Falls the Shadow
—T. S. Eliot

CHAPTER 1

Don't Make
a Career out of
the MS

May 12, 1986

N o question about it, Ms. Burstein," neurologist Labe Scheinberg tells me. "You have multiple sclerosis."

I am in a small examining room with bare walls at the Albert
Einstein College of Medicine's MS Care Center in New York City. It
looks like an army barracks, which is appropriate, because of the war
I am about to fight with multiple sclerosis.

Yet, oddly, I am relieved. My three-year quest to find out why my
left leg collapses when I run is finally over.

My husband, Brian, and my older sister, Karen, are with me in the
room. They are here for emotional support. They are also my witnesses in case I am told something I need to know but do not want to
hear.

But there is no reason for any of us to question this man or the diagnosis. Ordinarily, I ask a lot of questions. It is part of my job as an

investigative consumer reporter for a television station in Orlando, Florida. But without further inquiry, I accept Dr. Scheinberg's statements as fact.

The evidence is spread out on his desk next to the examining table. There are detailed reports from orthopedists and neurologists I previously consulted, along with the results of the lab tests.

As he reviews the data I study him, an elfin man with a gentle and friendly face. He speaks with a soft Southern accent. His manner is pensive, more like a professor's than a doctor's.

Scheinberg switches on a light box and holds up my MRI, a magnetic resonance imaging X ray. Pointing out the white areas at the top portion of my spinal cord, he says, "These are MS plaques."

The plaques (scars) are caused by the immune system going haywire—attacking itself and destroying the coating (myelin) that protects the nerve fibers in the brain and spinal cord. As a result, messages between the cells are short-circuited.

I already know that multiple sclerosis, a degenerative disease of the central nervous system, is characterized by exacerbations and remissions. Attacks leave scars in multiple places along the motor pathway. Hence the name multiple sclerosis. Where these scars form determines what function is affected. In my case it's the legs.

It is often difficult to diagnose MS because it mimics so many other conditions. Its moniker: the Great Imitator. In its most benign form MS causes minor inconveniences such as fatigue, tingling in the limbs, and heat sensitivity. At its worst it can lead to total paralysis, locking its victims into their bodies, rendering them unable even to communicate. There are many variations in between and every case is different.

The only certainty is that MS has a prognosis of a question mark. Although the research indicates that it is an autoimmune disease, no one knows what causes it. There is no cure.

I think multiple sclerosis is just two nasty little words that will give people like my cameraman, R. C. Lee, an explanation for why I lose my balance. It will no longer be amusing when he remarks, "Ellen, if there is a hole, you will find it and fall into it."

After Scheinberg tests muscle strength in my legs and arms, he concludes, "You have a slow progressive form of multiple sclerosis. While we can't predict what will happen, I think you'll do just fine."

He suggests I try Imuran, an immunosuppressive drug, to halt the progression. "Sixty percent of our patients have responded well to it," he reports. "But you'll have to get monthly blood tests so we can monitor your white blood count, platelets, and liver function. And I'll need to see you every three months."

Frightened as I am of needles, I agree it is worth a shot. I am not one who sits back and lets things happen to me. As Scheinberg says good-bye, he counsels, "Go back to Orlando. Go on with your life. Don't make a career out of the MS. Treat it like a minor inconvenience."

I like this man. He does not console. Instead he motivates. I will follow his advice willingly because I am accustomed to setting my own limitations, and I will not allow the MS to take over. At forty-one, I am not only functioning—I am flourishing, personally and professionally.

In the hallway I see several MS patients using wheelchairs and walkers. That is *their* future. It is not mine. Somehow the MS does not apply to me. Though there can be no denying that I have it, I refuse to acknowledge the damage it might cause.

In the elevator Brian and Karen are silent, and I am grateful. I need time to think about what I have just been told.

Once outside the hospital, where we wait for the driver to collect us, I break the silence. "I'm really glad I came here," I say, "because now that I know what's wrong I can fix it. And once the medicine kicks in, I'll be able to run again." They just smile at me.

The May air is mild and fresh, a perfect day for running. I see several people jogging around the perimeter of the hospital grounds, and I am heartbroken.

Running is a passion for a lot of reasons. I stopped smoking and started running three years ago when my father was diagnosed with lung cancer. In the final weeks of his life I would run forty blocks from my twin's apartment to his hospital room at Mount Sinai in New York

City. It was my way of distracting myself from the pain of watching my father in pain.

As I jogged into his room in my running shorts, T-shirt, and Nikes, he inquired in a faint voice, "Are you training for the Olympics?" He was amused by my sudden transformation into an athlete. Running was my first successful attempt at a sport.

As a fat, uncoordinated kid I was always the last to be chosen for my twin Patricia's baseball team. And she would be furious when, in frustration, I took the bat and left the field. *If I don't play,* I felt, *nobody plays.*

Eventually I returned the bat and took refuge in books. I would climb up the branches of a huge oak tree in our backyard and sit there with my loneliness, fantasizing I was as clever as Nancy Drew, solving mysteries, never giving in or giving up.

The last time I saw my father, before he slipped into an irreversible coma, was the day of the 1983 New York City Marathon. From the window of his hospital room we could see some of the competitors. "I'll be back," I told him, "to run next year's marathon."

"You can do anything you decide to do," he encouraged me. He died the next day.

Back in Orlando, grief, such a stealthy emotion, followed me everywhere. Just when I thought I was feeling better, I would turn a corner, have a remembrance, and weep. Running was my way of moving past my sorrow. I would look up at the stars and talk to my father about the events of the day.

My sister apparently sees my sadness. "Are you okay?" she asks and gently touches my shoulder.

"Sure," I answer. "Look at it this way—if I end up in a wheelchair I could be the Ironside of television reporting. And, besides, I always thought five feet was too tall; three feet is a much better height for me."

As we get into the car, Brian hugs me and whispers, "Are you scared?"

"No," I say. "It's no big deal." But, truthfully, deep inside I am very scared.

I know the diagnosis, which has taken thirty minutes, will alter my life irreparably and touch everyone close to me.

———

When we arrive at my mother's home on Long Island, Brian and Karen join the MS summit conference already under way in her sitting room. All but my youngest brother, Judd, are present—five delegates with five agendas. My mother, a New York State supreme court justice, presides.

I decide to go power walking, which I now have to substitute for running. Let them do the talking, I figure, and I'll come back in an hour to edit their conclusions.

Karen will present the facts of my MS. Translator par excellence, she manages to convey unwelcome news and make it less scary. She brings to this task a tremendous gift of language, wrapping unpleasantries in literary words and then packaging them in lawyerly logic.

It is about six o'clock in the evening when I head out to the back of Lawrence, walking quickly past large old Tudor- and Georgian-style homes set back from the street behind tall hedges and gravel driveways.

I grew up in this affluent village about an hour from New York City, and lived in a three-story, twenty-one-room Dutch Colonial house on two acres of land. It had fireplaces in every bedroom, high ceilings, hardwood floors, carved wooden banisters, pull-chain toilets, and bathtubs with ornate legs. By 1952, when I was seven, there were four girls and one boy, soon to be followed by the last child, a brother for him. Twelve years separate the oldest from the youngest.

Ours was a privileged childhood, with music lessons for each of us; a library that would eventually grow to more than five thousand books, most all of them read by one or another of us; and classical music permeating the house on Sunday mornings, the only day our father stayed home from his law office.

On Father's Day, instead of giving him ties and handkerchiefs, we performed trios for him: Karen on cello, Patricia on piano, I on violin, and our younger sister, Jessica, as page-turner and backup pianist. We were also the entertainment for my parents' dinner parties.

There were three people in household help, not for image, but rather for convenience. This allowed my mother to practice law and then campaign for judge. Besides, my father preferred that we spend our time reading and studying instead of doing household chores.

It was a house for children. There were no admonishments for fingerprints smudged on walls, stereos played at the highest decibel, or windowpanes broken by misguided baseballs. Punishment was reserved for the failure to complete homework and for bad report cards. The backyard was designed for fun. There was a log cabin, a miniature merry-go-round, a jungle gym, and a baseball diamond.

But all this privilege was not without pain. I was in constant conflict with my father, who admitted to me years later that he just did not like me as a child. He made me feel fat, stupid, and ugly, and set expectations that I could not meet.

Only recently have I come to understand that there can be no restitution for his emotional abuse. I accept that it happened and I move on. That is what I intend to do with the MS.

As I bend down to tighten the electric-blue laces on my jogging shoes, I am reminded of my blue suede loafers. At twelve, I convinced my parents to let me wear them instead of orthopedic saddle shoes and white bucks. While my friends stuck with the basics, brown penny loafers, I opted for Elvis Presley's favorite, blue suede.

I loved my loafers so much that I only took them off to sleep. When I wore them out in a few weeks, my parents insisted that I had to return to saddle shoe hell. Extremely upset, I threatened, "If you don't get me another pair of blue suede loafers, I will get very sick."

To my surprise and their horror I woke up the following day with tonsillitis and a high fever. That night my parents tiptoed into my room and left a gift-wrapped box. Inside was a new pair of blue suede loafers.

It was my first experience with mind over body. I also learned that illness has its own rewards: attention, stuffed animals, books, promises of trips, ice cream, and best of all, staying home from school.

But I am an adult now and I do not want to stay home from work.

My job as a television investigative consumer reporter allows me to point a camera and make a difference. A local newspaper columnist wrote that I am "the defender of the little guy—the righter of wrongs." I love my job and wonder if the MS will stop me from righting those wrongs.

And how will I explain my questionable future to my employer? Maybe if I don't call attention to my condition, no one will notice it.

As I walk up the driveway, I look up at my childhood house, a fortress against ill fortune. Nothing bad was ever supposed to happen to any of us. We were protected. Everything changed today.

The MS summit is still going on; everyone will want to be heard. I am not accustomed to being the focus of attention because, always, I have felt like an outsider. Because I felt so inadequate, my heart left home at an early age. And when I moved out after college, I left no traces of my childhood—not even my Raggedy Ann doll, pictures of high school boyfriends, or the oversized sweatshirts I wore to hide my chubby adolescent body.

Disengaging was my way of not getting lost inside this large family of powerful personalities. Later I became so self-absorbed that I ignored them. Now, all these years later, I do not know them and they do not know me. So how do I ask them for help? Is it fair for me to do so?

I stop at the sitting room door on my way to the bathroom. The family looks as though they were in mourning. In a cheery voice, I say, "I'll be right back. I just did two miles and I have to wash up."

When I return I sit next to Brian, who takes my hand and squeezes it. My mother is on the telephone. As I glance around the room, the MS is becoming more understandable. It is said to affect an unusually large number of women in the Northeast who have Type A personalities. The sitting room is a monument to this.

There is a picture of me, in jeans, sandals, sunglasses, and long hair, walking with President Gerald Ford at Camp David. I was there, in 1974, as a guest of the White House photographer. Next to this is a shot of Patricia interviewing Golda Meir. On the other walls there are photos of Karen on the campaign trail and of my brother Johnny dressed as his TV character, Slim Goodbody, a children's health ambassador. Judd, a lawyer, is represented in several family portraits, many of them taken by my younger sister, Jessica, a professional photographer.

When my mother gets off the phone, I smile and ask her, "So, what's new?"

In the last hour, I learn, my mother has been attending to the worst-case scenario. She has talked to her lawyer about changing her will to protect me when I become disabled. She has asked her financial adviser to set up a special trust for me. And she has summoned an architect to make the house wheelchair-accessible.

"Look, I really appreciate these plans," I tell her. "But didn't you notice that I just ran up the stairs? Please do not provide for a disability that doesn't exist."

She explains, "I am just trying to make sure that you will be taken care of when I am gone."

Jessica and Patricia challenge, "And just where do you think you're going?"

Frustrated, my mother proclaims, "*Please*, I'm seventy-one years old—I'm not going to be around much longer."

Patricia grins. "*Please*, Mother, you will outlive all of us."

Indeed, my mother is a remarkable woman of uncommon fortitude and wisdom. She doesn't look just at the moment but also at its possible consequences. This way she ensures there are no surprises and, invariably, disasters are preempted.

My mother continues. "It's a good thing your father is not here. He would be devastated."

Jessica, apparently upset, says, "The doctor doesn't know what he is talking about. You don't have MS!"

Johnny agrees with her that the doctor is wrong, but only about the name of the illness. My brother's diagnosis: I have ALS, a fatal illness known as Lou Gehrig's disease.

And from Patricia: "Don't worry, Ellen, you won't have to go into a nursing home. I'll look after you."

Oh, give me a break, I think, *this family is making me crazy.* Jessica wants more proof that I have something I don't want. Johnny wants me to make funeral plans. And Patricia has already turned me into an invalid and wants a new career as a nurse.

At this point Karen intervenes. "There is absolutely no question Ellen has MS. All the tests prove it."

Meanwhile, my husband, Brian, fascinated and amused by their various theories, remains a mere observer. He prefers it this way. In my family, he knows, in-laws are considered outsiders, or, as he puts it, outlaws. Moreover, he is in shock about the MS.

The summation belongs to me. "Look," I instruct my family, "don't panic. It's a minor problem that's going to go away. Let's forget it and have dinner."

It is back to old times at the dinner table with everyone shouting their opinions at each other about Iran-Contra, insider trading, and other topics in the news. But ignoring the MS will not make it go away. What remains unspoken is how their lives will change, because what happens to me will happen to them. Ultimately, they may have to adjust their lives to make mine more comfortable.

It is ironic that it is an illness that has brought me back to the family. But I am reassured that they care about me and will do everything possible to help.

After dinner Brian and I, who have to catch an early flight back to Orlando, say good night to everyone and go directly to bed. Just as I am falling asleep, Brian nudges me and says, "Ellen, remember our marriage vows: *in sickness and in health.* . . . Well, Ellen, I think you just used up all your sickness."

On the plane I repeatedly tell Brian that I don't want to discuss the MS anymore and, further, that he is not to let anyone know I have it.

At the baggage carousel in Orlando someone recognizes me from television and calls out, "Hi, Ellen, how are you doing?"

"Fine," I answer. "I have MS."

CHAPTER 2

Back to the Past

On my first day back at work I tell my employer, Mike Schweitzer, about the MS. Better to let him know, I figure, when I am in a position of strength. I give him pamphlets about MS and assure him that it's no big deal and I'll beat it. The literature, which claims that 75 percent of all MS patients remain ambulatory, backs me up. Mike says he is greatly pleased with my work and not to worry.

The timing of my MS confession is fortuitous. Several times a day, the TV station is running what it calls a "proof of performance" promotion about me. It is based on a series of reports I aired about a mobile home broker who cheated several people out of the profit from the sales of their trailers.

"This man didn't stand a chance," an ominous voice-over proclaims, "because Ellen MacFarlane was hot on his trail and she doesn't give up . . . she is *the* Action Reporter in Orlando."

I decided to use MacFarlane, my married name, when I moved here because it marked a new start for me. Also, Brian had previously worked as a news director in Orlando and I thought there would be some built-in name recognition.

I love this job because for the first time in my life I feel I am doing something useful and important. I am constantly appalled by the pain some people inflict on others out of greed and the camera allows me to shine a light on injustices and hold people accountable for their actions and behavior.

Close to a hundred distraught consumers call me every day about disreputable home builders, oleaginous used car salesmen, and bogus employment agencies, among other complaints. That's when I go into action, hunting down the scam artists and bringing them to justice on the six o'clock news. There are so many rip-offs that need to be exposed but only time enough to cover three a week. I try to choose the stories that are the most important to the most people without regard to the amount of monetary loss. Talmudic logic informs my work: "If you save one life it is as if you have saved the entire world."

It takes quick legwork to keep one step ahead of the crooks and swindlers and I am concerned that the MS may one day slow me down.

When I arrived in Orlando in 1981 there was no consumer watchdog and my size, five feet, one hundred and five pounds, gave me an advantage. If I were bigger it might appear that I bully the crooks I chase. Instead the viewers perceive me as the feisty defender of the fleeced. What I do is often the quickest way to right a wrong when there is little or no legal recourse.

I am, above all, very good at what I do.

———

Until recently, I could not have written the preceding sentence. It has taken me forty-one years to understand that I am a worthwhile human being.

I don't want to whine about my past. All the complaining in the world won't change it and I am not a collector of injustices.

In a few words, my father's constant criticisms annihilated my childhood. I believed he was right when he called me *stupid, lazy, a liar,* and *a cheat.*

Isn't it ironic that I now work sixty hours a week and win awards for exposing *liars* and *cheats.*

As a child I could not do anything right. I wanted to be invisible so my father would stop yelling at me. When I looked to my mother for comfort, it wasn't there. She was neither accepting nor rejecting. She was, simply, remote.

Every night I went to sleep praying that I would wake up and be a better person. Then, my father would be happy to see me. I couldn't just be myself, a pretty little girl with a friendly personality, which is what people outside the family said of me. That wasn't enough, and besides, I didn't believe them anyway. My father's opinion prevailed.

Whenever I looked into his deep blue eyes all I saw was an ice pick of cold scorn. Alone in my room, I'd hold on to my boxer dog, Kelly, and cry.

The son of poor Jewish immigrants, my father worked six and a half days a week and never took a vacation. He wanted to give his children every opportunity to learn and to flourish. Through the sheer force of his endurance, fierce intellect, and worldly wisdom, he succeeded brilliantly as an international lawyer.

So who was I, with my bad report cards, clumsy attempts at sports, and lack of a single talent, to question his pronouncements? And how could I, a mere child, possess the stamina and wherewithal to challenge him?

Though engulfed by a sadness that blurred much of my childhood, I do remember one shining moment. It was the day I learned to read. There I sat in kindergarten, holding a book with big black print and flowers etched at the top of the page, when I made a crucial connection. The words I read were the same as those people spoke. They were not separate entities.

It was a big moment for me and from then on books were my best friends, never letting me down. The more I read the easier it became to disengage from the bad and useless little girl so, for years, I always kept a book in my back pocket.

From his place at the head of the table my father ruled the world, correct in his opinions and certain that anyone who disagreed was a moron. My sisters tried, unsuccessfully, to cushion the effect of his unremitting diatribes against me. Instead their own successes only compounded my situation. I was overwhelmed by feelings of inadequacy. What did I have that was special? Nothing.

Karen, the oldest, was my father's intellectual clone and a serious and brilliant student. My twin, Patricia, got straight A's and was a natural athlete. The youngest, Jessica, beautiful, graceful, and artistic, was *Daddy's little girl.*

My brothers didn't affect me much. Judd, the youngest, was born when I was nine, after I had already emotionally separated from the family. Johnny only became an object of interest to me later on when my father began to transfer some of his disdain for me onto him. I empathized with Johnny and we became very close.

I was so jealous of Jessica that, at seven, I devised a plan to make her the victim of my father's wrath. Imitating her primitive, five-year-old penmanship, with *B* backward and *W* upside down, I wrote on doors and walls with a Magic Marker. For months she was blamed for defacing the house. Then I was caught in the act and it gave my father another reason to dislike me.

The Magic Marker episode was further proof that I was a terrible person. Although Jessica never blamed me for the distress I caused her, I was consumed by guilt and it would take more than thirty years for me to feel comfortable with her

Away from the family I made attempts at being special. In third grade, the top pupil each week wore a crown and was called king or queen. Despite being a precocious reader I was a poor student and was never chosen. One day, when another classmate was crowned, I produced the crown I had made at home, put it on, and acted like royalty.

However, my twin—part friend, part bully—was always there to remind me that I was not omnipotent. We shared a bedroom and almost every morning Patricia, who was born fastidious, launched a grouch attack about my bobby pins not being lined up perfectly on my bureau.

On school nights I would get into bed by ten but couldn't sleep because Patricia, who wanted to be a writer, would stay up banging away at her typewriter. One morning I got even with her. I set the alarm for 4 A.M., jumped out of bed, turned on all the lights, slammed doors, and put a record in the Victrola, turning it up to its highest volume. Patricia ceased her late night activities and morning verbal attacks. My first object lesson was a great success.

In high school my parents forbade us to wear lipstick or stockings. When I protested, "But everyone is doing it," they answered, "Not everyone, because you're not doing it." And if we got a bad report card there was no chance of going out on a date. Because of my poor grades I was pretty much grounded during those years.

At fifteen, Patricia and I went to Europe for the first time on a work-study program in Holland. Thus began an enduring romance with travel, disrupted only by my father's letters instructing me to write more often.

I now look on my childhood in much the same way as I regard my work. I do not care why someone cheated another person, only that it happened and somebody was hurt. Similarly with the MS. It is something that has happened and it doesn't matter why. If I know the *why*, what difference does it make? It's still there.

I graduated from high school in 1962. I left my childhood still in search of an identity, with no idea what I wanted to become. There was only one certainty—I did not want to be a mother.

I was afraid I might have a child I didn't like.

CHAPTER 3

Fast Forward

In the fall of 1962 I entered Carnegie-Mellon University in Pittsburgh, Pennsylvania. It was four years of exploration, self-discovery, and liberation. Admittedly, my friends and I passed through most of it in a haze of marijuana smoke while reading from *The Tibetan Book of the Dead*. We convinced ourselves that this extracurricular activity was mind-enhancing.

I was a terrible student. Mostly I read, played bridge, smoked dope, and led esoteric discussions in my dorm lounge about civil rights and the Vietnam War. No one suspected that my eloquence came from plagiarizing the thoughts expressed by Karen and my father at the dinner table.

Biology was my chosen major, but after failing math I switched to modern languages. Since I had spent the previous summer studying Spanish at the University of Mexico, I thought it would be easier.

It wasn't and my first-semester grade average hovered just above a D. My father came to Pittsburgh to talk to my professors. Since my best subject was cutting classes, none of them knew who I was.

The next semester a literature professor succeeded in engaging my attention. We were reading *The Stranger* by Albert Camus when he called on me to explain a passage. Being quite inarticulate, I kind of stumbled around trying to find the right words. To my amazement he said, "Ellen is absolutely right!" Then he rephrased what I had said and made it sound really intelligent. Because of his sensitivity, I learned to trust and to express my thoughts.

In my junior year I met Steven, a handsome drama student, who had thick wavy black hair and black eyes that sparkled with affection for me. Within days we were inseparable and during one afternoon walk, he suddenly asked, "Will you marry me?" I didn't know if he meant it, but I needed someone to love me. He did and he was kind and gentle. So I said, "Okay."

When I brought Steven home to meet my family, the response was polite disinterest mixed with caveats about the poverty that might befall me if I married an actor. I promised my parents that I would postpone marriage until after I graduated.

A few months before graduation I called my father and said, "I'm going crazy—I'm quitting school."

He was not very sympathetic. "No one in this family goes crazy," he hollered. "You're quitting over my dead body!"

When his anger subsided, he said something that continues to keep me going whenever I think of giving up. "Don't quit," he said, "if for no other reason than you should complete what you start. Don't quit. You will never regret finishing your education."

My father was right and he was also very relieved when the term ended and I graduated. Although I was still engaged to Steven, who had joined the U.S. Coast Guard to avoid the Vietnam draft, I was having second thoughts about marriage.

He was a terrific person, but he had limited acting talent and with his new military-style crew cut, he no longer looked like a gorgeous, up-and-coming movie star. I eventually called off the engagement and broke Steven's heart.

Without marriage as an escape, I had to figure out another getaway from the family. So I applied for a job as a flight attendant with my favorite airline, Pan Am. I scored one hundred on the written exam, but failed the height test and was disqualified.

What could I do? In those days, proficiency in typing and short-hand was required of women seeking employment. I had learned only two manual skills—and those were in my fourth-grade home economics class: how to make cinnamon toast and how to sew a hem.

I looked for work that allowed me to fill out forms by hand and found it at the New York State Unemployment Office. But my job as a counselor made no sense. I was supposed to tell people laid off from factory jobs in the summer to look for work. Instead, I'd advise them, "Take the summer off. When the factory reopens in the fall you'll go back to work."

I figured why should they go through the aggravation of looking for work when they already had a job. "No problem," I assured them. "Just come in every week to pick up your unemployment check."

Mr. Murray, my supervisor, became as alarmed by my largesse as by my forgetfulness about checking off a little box indicating whether an applicant was *Caucasian, Negro, Asian,* or *Other*.

Because I could never remember what race belonged to what person, when Mr. Murray instructed me to fill in the blanks, I'd just go "eenie, meenie, meinie, mo," randomly picking a race for each person. Three months later I decided to quit before I was fired.

My next job was more interesting, teaching reading and study skills at several private high schools and colleges around the country. The following year, 1967, I was accepted, on probation, at Columbia University's Teachers College. Through teaching others how to study, I had learned how to be a student. My first semester grades were all A's and B+'s and after one year I graduated with a master's degree in educational psychology.

Through Columbia's placement office, I got a job as an Assistant Professor and Reading Specialist at Federal City College in Washington, D.C. It was the nation's first land-grant college, created in the aftermath of the 1968 race riots. With its open admissions policy and yearly tuition of seventy-five dollars, it gave inner-city black students a chance to get a college education.

I had just read Claude Brown's *Manchild in the Promised Land,* which discussed why one person gets out of the ghetto and another doesn't. The author felt it was because of something a child reads, someone he or she meets, or a teacher.

I wanted to be that teacher and I gave my students books like *The Autobiography of Malcolm* X and *A Clockwork Orange* by the British writer Anthony Burgess to get them interested in reading. The latter was significant because the author made up words and it was the best way to show that you didn't have to know a word to understand its meaning.

During one of the weekly, EST-like faculty meetings, I learned something important about myself. As one of only a few white instructors, I greatly admired my black colleagues. They all had M.A.s or Ph.D.s and had worked hard to pay for their educations.

"You have all accomplished so much," I said. "I'm not sure I would be here if my father hadn't paid my graduate school tuition and expenses."

One of the black instructors interrupted me. "It doesn't matter, Ellen," he said. "You did it."

Years later I understood he was right. Yes, I had financial support, but I still did it and that's what counts. However, at that moment, my successes still belonged to my father. My failures were my own.

During that year I also lost thirty pounds and never gained them back. To go with my new svelte image, I bought a motorcycle, and in a miniskirt and with my long hair billowing in the wind, commuted to work on it.

I thought I was very cool and I was also quite popular with men. Once I was confident they were crazy about me, I'd drop them like twigs in a forest. It was my method, albeit unconscious, of getting revenge for the way my father treated me as a child.

After a year and a half in Washington, I wanted a change so I acquired another fiancé. I met David while on a long weekend on the Caribbean island of St. Thomas. He was blond and fairly handsome and when he asked me to marry him a few days after we met, it seemed to be the solution to my restlessness. Shortly after I returned to New York and David told me that he expected me to stay home, cook and clean, I broke our engagement.

Patricia, a newspaper reporter, had just quit her job so she joined me on a four-month honeymoon from work. We traveled to Eastern and Western Europe, Israel, and Iran. It was on this trip I found my calling.

At the Cannes Film Festival, I was invited to stay on a yacht rented by the now defunct Allied Artists Pictures. The producers, directors, and actors on board appeared to be really enjoying themselves. Suddenly I had an epiphany: *this is the life I want and if I can't be a singer or actress, I'll be a movie producer or director.*

When I returned home, I became a groupie for TV commercials, dating a few directors and getting occasional roles as an extra. I also began to learn the basics: how to shoot and edit film.

My new career almost ended when my older sister, Karen, decided to run for the U.S. Congress. All of us were recruited to work on the campaign. I, alone, refused. It was the bravest decision I ever made because my father raged at me about being disloyal and an ingrate.

Much as I wanted my sister to win, I had to think of my own career in showbiz. I wasn't getting any younger. I was twenty-five, already four years out of college, and not yet a movie director. If I didn't work on the campaign, my father said, I could not count on his financial support.

Within a week I moved into a studio apartment in New York and through an employment agency I was hired as the secretary for two talent coordinators on "The Tonight Show" with Johnny Carson. I got the job because I looked terrific sitting at a front desk in a miniskirt.

After my first week on the job, the producer thought my left arm was paralyzed because I typed with only one finger of my right hand. At that point I confessed, telling them I had a master's degree and although I couldn't type, I could read, which I thought was much more important.

They kept me on, despite my hopeless typing, because I did good preinterviews with guests. It was an interesting six months. One day a talent coordinator who was going out of town gave me her ticket to a party for Erich Segal, author of the best-selling *Love Story*. He was booked on the show the following week.

At the party, Erich Segal came over to talk to me and then, apparently unimpressed, walked away after a few minutes. A *New York Times* reporter then approached me. He was very friendly so I felt better. We chatted for a while about our respective jobs and in the course of conversation he remarked, "I saw you talking to Erich Segal. What do you think of him?"

Standing there, thin and glamorous in tight green velvet pants and a black leotard top, I guess I felt a little offended that Segal had slighted me. So I said his writing was sophomoric, adding, "I don't get the impression that he's crazy about women."

Shortly thereafter, an article about the author appeared in *The New York Times Magazine* and, to my utter surprise, it included the opinions of a "Tonight Show" representative. Although the reporter didn't use my name, there was no mistaking me. He described me down to my skin-tight green velvet pants and the cigarette in my hand.

I had no idea that talking to a reporter could get me in so much trouble. Patricia, a print journalist, had never mentioned this to me. Segal refused to come on the show until the talent coordinator called him with an apology.

I almost lost my job because of what I thought was just a friendly conversation. But I didn't really care because I was pretty bored.

I needed a more academic job in television. News seemed promising. After all, I had just learned about the power of the press.

————

I got my start in broadcast journalism when a friend introduced me to a free-lance network producer. He hired me as his assistant for the *Apollo 15* space launch. I was not aware that television news had casting couches until I checked into the hotel in Cape Canaveral, Florida, and learned my new employer had booked us into adjoining rooms.

Immediately, I locked my adjoining door. He was enraged and told anyone who would listen not to hire me. I put up with his nastiness because I was already there, it was a memorable event, and after the launch I would never have to countenance him again.

He tried to mete out a final punishment minutes before the *Apollo* liftoff. "Stay inside the control room," he commanded. "You can't go outside to watch the launch."

"Do you know what *fat chance* means?" I asked on my way out the door. I watched the launch and never saw or spoke to him again.

Fortunately, my work efforts had been noticed by a writer for United Press International (UPI). He recommended me for a job as a producer with Newsweek Broadcasting, a new television syndication service of the magazine. Every week, twelve stories were sent to fifty TV stations around the country, to be used as inserts in their newscasts.

Executive producer John Corporon hired me immediately because, as he later told me, "You came into the room running" and "You had balls." The latter observation probably had to do with the outfit, a long jacket barely concealing the hot pants I wore to the interview.

Affirmative action and my background were also an advantage. In the early seventies, when corporations were pressured to hire women, there was a scarcity of female broadcasters. The next best choice was educated women.

My first story was about a vanity publisher. When I finished it, I delivered twelve hundred feet of an interview to the film processing lab. In return, the lab delivered a twelve-hundred-dollar bill. My panic increased when I tried to edit the voluminous amount of film. In one of the shots the interview subject was holding a cigarette; in the next frame there was nothing in his hands.

From that costly mistake I learned to listen to cameramen who showed me how to produce and edit stories. During my two years at Newsweek Broadcasting, I put in twelve-hour days, a habit that has endured, and I worked with some of the best print journalists, among them Maureen Orth, Peter Benchley, Peter Bonventre, and Lynn Povich.

Among the stories I covered were the first freedom flights from

Cuba, the Watergate hearings, and the return of POWs from Vietnam. After years of imprisonment some of the returning POWs did not know how to resume their lives and it was so sad to see the sorrow and confusion in their eyes.

At the end of the first year, a male producer was hired for twenty thousand dollars, twice my salary. The feminist movement was in its infancy and "equal pay for equal work" became my mantra around the office. In order for me to achieve wage parity with my new male colleague, my job was expanded to include reporting.

However, my limited broadcasting experience did not include voice control and I yelled my stories into the microphone. When news directors complained, "Get that woman off the air," I was promptly dispatched to a voice coach. The invaluable lessons altered my ambitions and career direction. I believed that on-air reporting would make me special.

Shortly after I began my quest for fame, I was hired as a general assignment reporter for WVUE-TV in New Orleans. I shipped fifteen cartons of books, two thousand in all, to my new home. Six months later, I packed them up again because I did not want to live in a city that grew roaches the size of bats; was so humid I couldn't get a comb through my frizzy hair; and had a celebration called Mardi Gras.

Before I left, in August 1974, Vice President Gerald Ford came to New Orleans and I was assigned to cover his speech. Standing next to me on the press platform was a charming and handsome *Time* magazine photographer named David Kennerly. I turned down his dinner invitation because I was packing for a move to Dallas and my new job as the medical and entertainment reporter for WFAA-TV.

The next day, Nixon resigned and Ford assumed the presidency. When David became the White House photographer, I sent a congratulatory note and, in November, accepted his invitation to spend a weekend in Washington, D.C.

Upon my arrival on a Friday evening, David greeted me with an apology I could not refuse. "There has been a last-minute change of plans," he said. "I have to work all weekend. Do you mind going to Camp David?"

We spent a day with President Ford and First Lady Betty Ford, who was recuperating from breast cancer surgery. When she learned I was a medical reporter, she asked me to look at a story that was to be published in a national women's magazine. Mrs. Ford felt it did not reflect her feelings about the ordeal and she enlisted my help to try to restore her voice to the article.

Throughout the weekend, first at Camp David and then in her private quarters inside the White House, we discussed her thoughts on the trip from the hospital bed to the operating room; what it meant to lose a breast; and her concerns about the future.

When I returned to Dallas I worked round-the-clock for two days writing the revised story. When the First Lady reviewed the changes, she sent me a letter of thanks, stating that she was thrilled with the results, which sounded so much more like her. When the article appeared, it was word-for-word what I had written.

Until now, I have not spoken of this. But that experience showed me the importance of finding my own voice so, like Betty Ford, I can speak from the heart in my writing.

While working in Dallas, I interviewed extraordinary people like the renowned heart surgeon Dr. Michael DeBakey. I stood beside him as he performed a coronary bypass operation. After he removed the heart-lung machine, the patient's heart began to fibrillate. With fierce concentration, DeBakey kept looking, back and forth, from the EKG monitor to his patient. I immediately left his operating room because he did not need any distractions and what he was doing was critical, much more important than any story.

The next day DeBakey called to thank me and invite me to his office for an in-depth interview. Best of all, his patient survived.

I also won the Texas State Medical Award for a cancer series and an Emmy for my report on a kidney transplant operation. And, much to my surprise, a magazine writer wanted to interview me for a feature headlined "THE TEN SEXIEST WOMEN IN DALLAS."

A dubious distinction, I thought, and initially declined. But I changed my mind after he explained that *sexy* meant *powerful* and, further, a sixtyish woman would be part of the round-up.

The day of the interview a photographer showed up at my apartment with a hairdresser and a makeup artist. The wardrobe they had in mind for the shot sounded suspiciously like lingerie. I, who lived in blue jeans and turtlenecks, compromised by posing in a neck-to-ankle white wool dress, covering my chest with my Yorkshire terrier, Adam, and posing in front of my two-thousand-book library. The published article was flattering.

About eight months into the job, I was unaware I had slowed down and was not being productive. But the news director had noticed my inertia and instead of asking what was causing it, left a note on my desk in full view of everyone in the newsroom.

"You are no longer the medical and entertainment editor," his note stated. "You are now a weekend general assignment reporter." It was a demotion.

I left a note on his desk: "I will not be working weekends or any other shift—I quit!"

At the time this struck me as a clever and appropriate response. He saw it as a bad attitude and in future years I was haunted by the animosity he felt for me and conveyed to prospective employers.

A few weeks later, I moved my difficult self to San Diego and a job with KGTV. Again, my dual beats were medicine and entertainment. But, this time, the major medical story turned out to be my own health.

I had forty-eight hours of excruciating pain before a gynecologist realized I was bleeding internally from a ruptured ovarian follicle. I went into surgery with a collapsed lung and needed four blood transfusions.

When I woke, I saw my father at my bedside. He was crying, the first time I had ever seen him do this. My mother then took his place for the remainder of my weeklong hospital stay. And during my six-week recuperation, Patricia and my brother Johnny came to San Diego to keep me company and entertain me.

Johnny gave me a private preview of the musical show he had created for his health-crusading character, Slim Goodbody. I had no idea until then that he was so talented. Within the year Slim Goodbody became a regular feature on the children's TV show "Captain Kangaroo."

When I returned to work, I went to a lab to film a report on a new procedure that analyzed blood tests in eight minutes. Because they were unable to find a patient to be a blood donor for the story, I volunteered. Eight minutes later I learned the hospital transfusions had given me serum hepatitis. Everyone in the newsroom rushed out to get a gamma globulin shot and I spent another month at home acquiring a yellow tint from jaundice.

When I recovered, a friend gave me a weekend pass to a health ranch just across the Mexican border. This got me hooked on aerobic exercise and I became a weekend regular at the place.

But just when I was starting to feel healthy, I began to experience strange seizure-like sensations. While they lasted only about ten seconds, they recurred every twenty minutes: my eyes lost focus, the upper left side of my lip curled, my speech slurred, and the left side of my face drooped.

I consulted Dr. Robert Nichols, a neurologist in La Jolla. When I discovered that his brother was Mike Nichols, the movie and stage director, I brought the doctor my TV movie review scripts for us to discuss after my EEG tests.

When lab tests eliminated a tumor, Dr. Nichols wanted to do a spinal tap. I refused because I had just accepted a job with WABC-TV in New York City and didn't have time for more tests. I asked him if I could try Dilantin, a drug used to control epilepsy. Within days of taking this medicine, the seizures stopped and Dr. Nichols said he did not know what caused them or if they would be a problem in the future.

In retrospect, I'm amazed that, as a medical reporter, it never occurred to me that the seizures were caused by multiple sclerosis. Ten years later, in 1986, when an Orlando neurologist suspected MS, I asked Dr. Nichols for my medical records. His diagnosis: possible demyelinating disease (multiple sclerosis).

I'm grateful that Dr. Nichols did not tell me he suspected MS because, then, it would have been like a death sentence. I would have surrendered to it because I was still grasping at my life and did not have the inner strength to move past an illness like MS. Besides, what could I have done about it? Sit down and wait for an attack? This time, with the Dilantin, I had lucked out. I was on my way to New York to the number-one station in the number-one market.

But the MS followed me to New York. I didn't know why I was constantly fatigued, experiencing vertigo when I made rapid movements, and racing to gas station bathrooms between reporting assignments. Apparently, I was having one exacerbation after another, and unable to pinpoint what was wrong with me, began to feel confused and depressed.

I worked at a frantic pace, trying to overcome the discomfort. I chased Rosalynn Carter through Kennedy Airport for a comment about her husband's *Playboy* interview ("I've looked on a lot of women with lust. I've committed adultery in my heart many times . . .") and rushed to the scene of five-alarm blazes, gas explosions, and murders of junkies in the Bronx, between covering New York's infamous parades for every ethnic group known to mankind.

In 1976, advocacy journalism was in vogue. Reporters were supposed to become part of their stories and show strong emotion. In essence, I was supposed to *kick down unlocked doors*. I never felt comfortable with this news philosophy and could not understand why it was important for viewers to know what I thought about a story.

When the news director said I must develop a style, I inquired, "Why can't my style just be that I'm smart?"

"You're a woman in television," he said. "Smart isn't enough."

Style or no style, I had a certain presence at City Hall. Because I was about the same height as the diminutive New York Mayor Abe Beame, cameramen used me as a kind of human tape measure to position their lights before he entered the room for a press conference.

Back at the station I outsmarted myself because, so sure was I of my importance, I refused to sign a five-year contract. The station manager refused to negotiate and decided, "No contract, no job." We agreed that I would free-lance for them until I found another job. I left there a few months later, all the wiser for having learned to write quickly and succinctly in order to cover two or three stories a day.

There was one story that made me realize that I could point a camera and make a difference. One bitterly cold winter evening, I was sent out to cover a landlord-tenant dispute. The tenant was a ninety-three-year-old woman who had been living in her run-down apartment without water, gas, or heat for six weeks.

The report I aired showed her confusion and distress. To my amazement and delight, the following morning five New York City agencies had dispatched workers to her apartment. Within a few hours, all the basic services were restored.

In the fall of 1977, I began working in Atlanta at WXIA-TV as the noon anchor and entertainment editor. After work, I turned into a *Saturday Night Fever* disco queen and wore skirts slit up the side to reveal a lot of leg as I whirled around the dance floor on spike heels.

By the late seventies, Atlanta was a vibrant city with all the cultural amenities—symphony, theater, museums—I had become accustomed to growing up in New York. I reviewed movies and interviewed all the celebrities who passed through on promotion tours. Among them: Mr. Saturday Night Fever himself, John Travolta; The Fonz, Henry Winkler; and Joan Rivers.

After two years, when my contract came up for renewal, my employer refused to promote me to the weeknight anchor desk or give me a raise. I gave notice I was leaving as soon as I found another job. Nothing less than a full-time anchor position would do. As Dan Rather once wrote about television anchors, "It's a cheap way to be in the movies."

I had to settle for overnight anchor at the fledgling Cable News Network (CNN). I began work a month before its first newscast and quit two weeks after my first night on the air.

CNN headquarters in Atlanta was not yet completed and it was difficult to reach the Porta-Johns to accommodate my overactive bladder between fifteen-minute on-air recitations of the news. I was also intimidated by the sophisticated computer system and, as a morning person, I couldn't get used to ending my day at dawn.

I continued to work for CNN as a free-lance anchor while searching for the elusive prime-time anchor job. I found it with my former employer in San Diego. But within a week of accepting his offer, I realized that I didn't want to leave Atlanta. True to form, when I needed an out, I either got engaged or traveled. So when Jay, a chiropractor I had been dating, proposed marriage, I accepted.

It was a terrible decision that resulted in severe career damage when I told the San Diego employer, who had mounted a publicity campaign about my return to the station, I had changed my mind and no longer wanted the job.

My engagement, meanwhile, lasted only a few weeks, until Jay and I admitted to each other that while we had a great friendship, we were not in love.

After the latest job debacle, I decided to travel again, this time to China. Prior to leaving on the trip, I stopped in New York to see my parents and a friend and former Newsweek Broadcasting colleague, Sally Hunter. She was now the executive producer and had recently hired a senior producer, Brian MacFarlane. After Sally introduced us, Brian and I had a brief discussion about the news business and my impending trip to China. I didn't know I was talking to my future husband.

While I didn't have many fans in the United States, in China I found an enthusiastic audience who applauded when they saw Westerners. China had only recently opened up and I was one of the first tourists they met. I, in turn, was captured by the curiosity, generosity, and warmth of the Chinese people. When I saw the outline of Canton from the hydrofoil, I could not remember feeling so excited about anything in a long time. Here I was in a heretofore forbidden place. What an adventure!

I began every morning of my six weeks there watching the Chinese do t'ai chi. The graceful, flowing movements cleansed their minds and bodies and prepared them for the day.

I stood on part of the Great Wall, walked through the Forbidden City, traveled by boat along the Yangtze River, attended the first Mass at the newly reopened Catholic church in Peking, and was mesmerized by the moon in Hangchow. It was the largest one I had ever seen.

The Chinese are right in their belief. To paraphrase: "There is heaven above and Hangchow and Soochow below."

When I returned to Atlanta, I met and fell madly in love with Marty, a bright, talented, witty, and observant man, a network producer. His warning, "I'm very passionate in the beginning of a relationship, but I eventually lose interest," did not worry me. But two months later, he lived up to his self-description and ended the relationship. I was devastated.

The abandonment I had felt so deeply as a child colored my thinking and I didn't believe Marty when he said, "Just because I'm not madly in love with you doesn't mean I don't care about or like you." To me, if you no longer loved someone it also meant you didn't like them and never wanted to see them again.

I was unemployed and unloved, and my life began to unravel and disintegrate. Believing I'd do better as a blonde, I dyed my hair the day before flying to Boston for a job interview. Before boarding the plane, I stopped at a photo booth and posed for mug shots. When the machine spit out four pictures, I didn't recognize myself, thin and pale as an anorexic. No one, I thought, could possibly look this sad. The interviewer was not impressed with me or my hair.

When I arrived home, I lost the tenuous grip I had on my life. I began to weep and I couldn't stop. Until now, I had used work to anesthetize myself, much the same way people rely on drugs and alcohol.

I had no reason to go on living. My parents, hearing the futility in my voice, convinced me to see a psychiatrist. I found one I trusted. With no work, at least my daily appointments with him gave me a reason to get out of bed each morning.

After a month of therapy, my suicidal thoughts retreated and I was starting to feel more in possession of myself. At that point, the doctor suggested I think about looking for work.

I decided it was worth another try.

CHAPTER 4

Dear Mommy
and Daddy

On December 1, 1980, I arrived at the Radio and Television News Directors Convention in Hollywood, Florida, to look for a job. My friend Sally Hunter let me use the Newsweek Broadcasting booth as a base, so I wouldn't look like a displaced, unemployed reporter.

Brian MacFarlane, the senior producer I'd met recently in New York, was also there. He offered to introduce me to prospective employers and I agreed to meet him for an after-dinner drink.

Brian, wearing faded jeans and a raw silk designer sports jacket, greeted me with a winsome smile. He seemed comfortable with himself and in command of his life.

I was immediately attracted to this bright, funny, and athletic-looking man. Because his father had worked in the State Department, Brian had lived in Europe until he graduated from high school, where he had set a track record for sprinting.

After college, Brian went directly into television news, first as a reporter-cum-producer, eventually moving up to news director for stations in various cities. He was a year younger than I and divorced. He had two daughters: Tori, seven, and Amy, five, with whom he spent almost every weekend.

After looking at the videotape I'd brought to show prospective employers, Brian said I had extraordinary talent. Although this was his way of getting me to spend the night with him, I also believe he did see something in me that no one else did. Because I was so needy and grateful for his encouragement and approval, I moved into his hotel room for the duration of the convention—five days.

Three days after we began our passionate love affair, Brian asked me to move to Connecticut and live with him. When I explained that I had never lived with anyone before and was not going to start at age thirty-five, he proposed marriage.

On December 10, 1980, ten days after we met, Brian and I stood in front of the fireplace in his Connecticut apartment and were married by a justice of the peace. It was wonderful to get married while I was still falling in love and believed that the success of a marriage was not predicated on the length of the courtship.

When I told my family that I had eloped, they accepted it with equanimity. Aware of my fragile emotional condition, they were reluctant to challenge my impulsive decision. Besides, it was a fait accompli, and I was legally an adult. My parents' one dictum: I continue psychiatric treatment and send them the bill.

When I married Brian, I dropped out of the job market and my parents were supporting me for the first time since I had graduated from college. We lived in Guilford, a suburb of New Haven, which had a Currier & Ives look.

But my marital happiness was short-lived. I had no friends and felt isolated. I drove Brian to the train station in the morning and then spent the day reading, listening to music, and taking long walks; in the evening, I drove back to the train station to pick him up. Weekends, I entertained his children while he played golf. Every time I turned on the radio and heard Sheena Easton singing "My Baby Takes the Morning Train." I was reminded of my useless life.

Fortunately, Brian was a tidy person, because straightening up the house was not my forte. Cooking was also on the list of things I didn't know how to do. After I grilled a cheeseburger on both sides and made pancakes that looked as hard and pitted as a golf ball, Brian and I dined in on take-out meals.

I had given up on my job search because I could not face another rejection. I free-lanced as a producer for Newsweek Broadcasting and began writing a suspense novel about a television news viewer who murders an anchorwoman. It was a take-off on *The Fan,* a novel about an actress and an obsessed fan who fantasizes that he is her lover. When she ignores his letters, his love becomes hate and he tries to kill her.

I planned to use some of the quirky and obscene letters I had received from strangers when I was on the air. But I never even completed the book proposal because I was having trouble concentrating. Depression flattened my imagination and ambition. I was so paralyzed by despair that after only six months of marriage, I wanted a divorce from life.

Late one evening, after Brian had gone to bed, I sat alone in the living room with my sorrow. After six years and six jobs in six different cities my peripatetic self had ended up nowhere with no future and no purpose. It was time to end the pain.

I wrote farewell letters to my parents, Brian, and Patricia . . .

Dear Mommy and Daddy:

I'm so sorry to do this to you, but I can't go on. If you blame yourselves then I'll never have the peace I'm seeking. I've always known from the time I was a child that this is how my life would end. It's time for me to go.

I wish it were an illness that would justify this act. Please understand that I have to do this. No job, no psychiatrist, no amount of love can help. *Please, please, please,* be kind to Brian. He's the main reason I've stayed around so long after my breakdown.

Nothing is worth the pain I feel almost every moment.

I love you both very much! Please help Patricia get through this. I really care about how everyone accepts what I've done and *under-*

stands. No one person or thing is responsible. I'm a coward and I can't face another day.

Please give my body to science and any organs that are functional to people who need them. Maybe I can redeem myself this way if there is a God. I know there's a hell—I'm living it!

Also, give my possessions away and any funds I have to Patricia. Tell Karen, Patricia, Jessica, Johnny, and Judd I love them and I'm sorry. Please don't be sad. This has been inevitable.

Be happy I'm finally free of me.

Love,

Your daughter, always

Ellen

Dear Brian:

Please forgive me for what I felt I had to do. You are the only thing of joy in my life. But I just can't find peace.

It is nothing you have done or said. I've been a walking time bomb for a year and it was unfair of me to marry you.

I do love you as much as I can anyone. But no matter how much you could give it would never be enough.

I am really scared as I sit here writing, but what I'm doing is inevitable.

Love,

Ellen

Dear Patricia:

I'm sorry.

Please forgive me.

I love you.

Your twin

I left the notes on the coffee table, removed 50 milligrams of Valium from the medicine cabinet, and opened a bottle of Beaujolais. I left the apartment, walked down a flight of stairs and across the driveway to the garage where my Datsun 280Z was parked. After shutting the garage door, I sat down in the driver's seat, rolled up the windows, locked the doors, turned on the ignition, swallowed the Valium, drank the entire bottle of wine, and crouching in the darkness, told God I was very scared and hoped he would forgive me.

I survived because I didn't know it was necessary to run a hose from the exhaust into the Datsun. I was furious when I woke up at 5 A.M. I couldn't even succeed at suicide! Staggering back to the apartment, I fell asleep on the floor.

When Brian woke up and found me, he held me in his arms and carried me into the bathroom to bathe me. He called my psychiatrist and my parents, both of whom suggested I commit myself to a hospital for psychiatric treatment. I promised them I wouldn't try to hurt myself again and made an appointment to see the psychiatrist the next day. Brian then put me in bed to sleep off the wine and Valium.

The following morning, I discussed my failed suicide with my psychiatrist, Dr. Frank Ninivaggi. "Why did you do it?" he asked me.

"I wanted to find the white light."

"But you won't find it that way," he said. "People who have had life-after-life experiences after attempting suicide have found themselves in darkness, surrounded by terrifying images."

That was enough reason for me not to kill myself. Although suicide is the second leading cause of death for those with MS, this stops me from ever taking my own life.

I agreed to commit myself to a psychiatric hospital if my depression persisted. It did. I paced all day, my hands shook from anxiety, and my weight dropped to ninety pounds.

A few days after the failed suicide, Brian surprised me with a shih tzu puppy. I named my beautiful little six-week-old puppy Churchill. We took him to the park for a walk and when he licked my face and fell asleep in my arms, it seemed unimaginable that there could be so much pain in my world. To disturb this puppy's innocence and delight would be an act of extraordinary cruelty. I started to sob. I couldn't stop.

I was crying for my childhood.

CHAPTER 5

I Am Not a Happy Camper

August 1981

Why are you following me?" I ask the attendant who stands beside the toilet I am sitting on. She has not left my side since I checked into the Elmcrest Psychiatric Institute in Portland, Connecticut, this morning.

"You're on suicide watch," she informs me.

"Believe me," I explain, "it's impossible to urinate and kill yourself at the same time. Besides, I'm not going to kill myself. Please leave me alone."

I am reminded of "The Shadow," the weekly radio suspense program I listened to on my red transistor radio when I was twelve. "Who knows what evil lurks in the hearts of men . . . The Shadow knows." Only this time "The Shadow" is a huge attendant with vacant eyes who stalks me, ferreting inside my suitcases for scissors and

other sharp objects and removing all but the ten cigarettes I'm allowed daily.

Elmcrest is a large private facility, with neo-Gothic redbrick build-
ings spread out over several acres of land like bunks at summer camp.
There is an outdoor swimming pool but it is covered with algae float-
ing on the surface like green Jell-O.

I am not a happy camper. I was sent to a crafts class to make a
hideous clay ashtray I don't need for only ten cigarettes a day. There
is no individual therapy, only group sessions with preppie substance
abusers and a seventeen-year-old boy who stabbed his parents. I have
nothing in common with these inmates—save for enough insurance
to cover our respective stays.

What am I doing here? I'm not crazy. I'm out of here. I call Dr. Ninivaggi and he calls off my "Shadow."

I ask permission to take a walk. "No," the "Shadow" barks, "that's
a reward you have to earn." I tell the chief shrink that his uncompro-
mising rules are created for crowd control, not for quelling a patient's
despair, that I expected individual, not group, therapy, and further,
his program will impede, not facilitate, my recovery.

"The next time your group meets," he says with a smug, intransi-
gent look, "let's talk about your anger."

Now I am really furious. Why did I bother to sit up half the night
in a garage trying to kill myself? All I had to do was come here and
talk to this nauseating man who issues orders in a thin, funereal voice.
I tell him I am leaving.

"You can't," he responds. "You have to stay at least two weeks."

The anguish of the past few weeks closes in and I begin to cry with
such intensity that I hyperventilate, my fingers contract into fists, and
my heart rate shoots up to 160. It takes about forty-five minutes for
me to calm down.

The following day, at a gathering of patients and staff, I let loose
about the way Elmcrest is run and how they only care about patients
until the insurance is up.

"I can tell you are a good reporter," the session leader remarks.

Now she's the news director! Maybe she has a job for me. Let me out of this jail! The boy who stabbed his parents belongs here—not me!

Our group session begins with an announcement that a teenage patient has hanged herself. We had been roommates my first night at Elmcrest and although she had attempted suicide several times and was semicatatonic from depression, she had not been put on suicide watch. I am astounded! If they hadn't been so busy following me to the toilet, they might have recognized how much trouble she was in. Even I could see it.

After gratuitous assurances from the staff about protecting us from self-inflicted death, a therapist asks, "Are there any questions?"

I have one: "Why is there a man on the floor in a straitjacket?"

From an attendant: "How insensitive of you to dismiss what happened to that poor girl!"

"Let me tell *you* something," I challenge. "That young woman committed suicide because you weren't watching her. So don't try to sidetrack the issue by attacking me. My concern is that this guy in the straitjacket has been screaming since we came in here and his hysteria frightens me. I want to know when you are going to free him."

As I speak these words, I realize I do not need to be here. I am obviously strong and healthy enough to gather my thoughts and articulate them. I call Brian and my parents to advise them of my intention to leave.

They tell me Dr. Ninivaggi thinks I need to stay at least one more week and they'll see me Saturday for a family counseling session.

The Elmcrest Psychiatric Institute is big on family reunions and it is high drama when my parents arrive. As my father walks toward me, I stand, shoulders hunched, prepared for battle. When he tries to kiss me, I pull away, yelling, "Just leave me alone!"

He begins to cry, saying, "It's all my fault." We go into the therapist's office and I think this is the time for truth. I tell him how he made me feel inadequate and stupid as a child and I hated myself because he hated me and I'd never be in this situation if it weren't for him and a part of me will always be dead.

My father says again it is all his fault and tells me he just didn't like me as a child and he couldn't control his rage. Too bad, I think, now *he* is the one who is scared.

When he and my mother agree with the therapist that I should stay at Elmcrest, I rage at both of them. "Don't you dare tell me I can't leave. This is all your fault!" The session ends and I stalk off, bellowing at my parents, "Don't ever talk to me again!"

I feel this enormous relief at raising my voice at my parents. Just getting out the years of anger frees me.

At the end of the second week the Elmcrest wizards warn me that I'll never make it if I leave and that they intend to get a court order to keep me there. Brian and my older sister, Karen, a lawyer, plead my case. With the backing of my parents, she threatens legal action if they do not release me. They relent.

The chief shrink's farewell message: "You will never fully recover if you choose to leave now. You will attempt suicide again."

I disagree. I choose life. There is no other choice. It's a Catch-22 situation. I still do not know how I will continue my life but I can't kill myself because I won't find the white light.

Maybe some morning I'll wake up and be glad I didn't die in that garage.

When I left the hospital, I told Brian I had to find a job as soon as possible. Since he had no great desire to remain in New York or at his job, he agreed to go wherever I found work.

In September 1981, at the annual Radio and Television News Directors Convention, in New Orleans, the news director for WFTV in Orlando, Florida, offered me a job as the Action Reporter (a TV consumer watchdog). Although the salary, seventeen thousand five hundred dollars, was not even a quarter of what I had earned previously, I was grateful for the chance to resuscitate my career.

Brian quit his job at Newsweek Broadcasting and with a loan from my father planned to start a production company. We flew to Orlando on a reconnaissance trip to find a place to live. I had second thoughts as soon as we left the terminal. The heat was stifling and our suitcases were covered by thousands of disgusting tiny flying insects called lovebugs. Traveling in pairs, they mated and smashed into every object in their path—leaving behind an acidic liquid that eats through even car paint.

Brian and I stayed in a dark, drab room in a cut-rate motel until we found a house to rent. We overlooked the revolting decor and pea-green carpet because it had four bedrooms and was affordable. Besides, however drastic the lifestyle changes, it had to be better than confinement at Elmcrest.

I found an excellent psychiatrist to see three times a week. The Myth of Sisyphus statue in his office reminded me of the futility I still felt. Now that I had made a decision to continue my life, I just needed to find out what was so great about living and how to feel joy.

During my first three months as an Action Reporter, I covered run-of-the-mill consumer complaints: leaky roofs, sloppy car repairs, and faulty televisions and stereos. I began to do more substantive work with an investigation of slum landlords in low-income black communities. This also marked the start of an enduring professional relationship and friendship with cameraman R. C. Lee.

As I examined thousands of complaints filed with the Orlando Minimum Housing Department, one name kept reappearing. Owen Manning was a property manager for five hundred houses, most of them in need of repairs. At least twenty of them were unlivable: rat-infested, without electricity, with broken windows and doors.

His terrified tenants told me every time they complained to the Housing Department, Manning raised their rent ninety-five to two hundred dollars a month.

This enraged me and when Manning refused to return my calls, I went to his office to confront him. R.C. and I, camera rolling and microphone in hand, marched past the protesting receptionist and through the open door of his inner office. Owen Manning glared at us.

"Hello, Mr. Manning," I said. "I'm Ellen MacFarlane from Channel 9. Several of your tenants tell me you refuse to repair their houses. Why don't you correct the serious health and safety violations?"

I was about to ask how he could be so inhumane and indecent when he suddenly stood up and came out from behind the desk. Owen Manning, a white man in his early forties, was huge, well over six feet, and about two hundred and fifty pounds. Hands raised to block the camera, he charged at us, yelled, "Get out of here," and shoved R.C. and me out the door.

We got it all on tape. I was on the air that evening at six:

> Numerous property owners of rental homes in downtown Orlando have repeatedly been cited for serious housing code violations.
>
> If city officials read the complaints carefully, they would realize many of the problems are caused by one property manager.
>
> Meet Owen Manning, a slum landlord who lives off the misery of people who can't fight back . . .
>
> I'll check to make sure the violations are corrected. I'll let you know.

I had decided to end many of my reports with "I'll let you know" because I wanted the crooks, victims, audience, and politicians to know that I would stay on a story until an injustice was corrected, even if it took months or years.

Within weeks of my report on Owen Manning, I let viewers know that the county's Minimum Housing investigators had helped relocate tenants after condemning several of his properties. Further, the Code Enforcement Board ordered Manning to repair other rentals immediately.

The 1982 Florida Associated Press Award I won for the slumlord series was nice, but not nearly as gratifying as knowing I had made a difference. As a result of my reports, a new law was enacted making it illegal for landlords to raise the rent when a tenant complained about repairs not being done and landlords were no longer allowed four months with numerous extensions to make corrections. It was now two months, no extensions, with heavy fines if deadlines were ignored.

This series was not the only one that resulted in new or better laws. The burgeoning time-share industry was my next target. Victims called me daily to complain about the high-pressure sales tactics.

Predatory time-share salespeople, offering valuable gifts, fanned out at beaches and lured tourists and Central Florida residents into listening to their spiel about vacation units. Other prospective buyers received urgent telegrams advising them that they could only claim their prizes by visiting a time-share resort with no obligation to purchase.

Once hooked, they were crunched together in tiny, noisy, airless rooms and made to feel like cheapskates and dopes if they didn't take advantage of this FANTASTIC ONCE-IN-A-LIFETIME OPPORTUNITY! to buy a two-week vacation unit at a special price offered only to them, right now . . . Hurry up . . . this moment . . . you won't get this chance again . . .

Those who succumbed were then railroaded into waiving their right to cancel the contract within three days. New time-share owners were exhausted and confused when they left the salesrooms. They were stunned and disgusted when they picked up their valuable gifts: a *big screen television set* was a cardboard box with a plastic magnifying glass; a *diamond and gold pendant* was gold-plated with a diamond chip the size of the head of a pin; and a *35mm camera*, made of flimsy plastic, took out-of-focus pictures.

My reports led to new time-share regulations that included a mandatory ten-day cooling-off period before a contract was valid. And the Florida Attorney General ordered several resorts to cease and desist their misleading and deceptive gift promotions.

Thus began my career as a pest and consumer vigilante. I began to pursue amoral creeps and curtail or end their activities. Among the rogues: unlicensed contractors who took thousands of dollars for work they never did; aluminum siding salesmen who convinced poor, illiterate homeowners and lonely senior citizens to sign contracts they couldn't read or understand and which required a second mortgage to pay for the work; and employment agencies collecting fees for illusory jobs.

Sometimes my stories ended with restitution for the victims and the culprits left town or went to prison. At the very least, I warned the public about bad people and bad deals.

After six months at the TV station I was asked to consider changing my Action Reporter beat for the noon anchor position. Without hesitation, I declined. The anchoring job I had once chased and coveted now held no appeal. I liked the *legwork*, being out in the field, instead of stuck behind a desk. I am a working reporter, a job I love and perform well.

No longer do I define myself by what I do in television. Rather, it's the *how* and *why* I do it that matters. It comes from my heart.

I was beginning to feel better about myself and my future. But, at home, Brian was having a difficult time. Every evening he was spoon-feeding me approval and confidence and with his news director's eye helping me to develop a strong on-air presence and a reputation as a solid reporter. Still, he was not prepared for his heretofore depressed wife's metamorphosis into an energetic, driven woman who frequently worked until midnight and on weekends. I, on the other hand, was inadvertently ignoring him and our marriage.

Brian soon began to suffer from a failure of will, spending more time playing golf than building a client list for his fledgling production company. Apart from his child support, I was paying all the bills. It was the first time I had to worry about money and I was frustrated by Brian's apparent lack of concern and initiative. I did not want to be responsible for his financial future.

My discomfort increased that summer when Brian's daughters, Tori and Amy, stayed with us for six weeks. They were really sweet and well behaved, but I was not used to having two little girls hover over me when I put on makeup, brushed my hair, and dressed for work. Still, I tried very hard to make them feel wanted and welcome.

A few nights after the girls left, Brian and I discussed our deteriorating marriage. He told me he felt unloved. I said his lack of productivity and failure to contribute financially were causing me to lose respect for him.

When I came home from work the next day, Brian was gone. He had left a note: "I'm in your way. You'll do better without me." Suddenly, I realized how thoughtless and careless I had been about his needs. It had never occurred to me that he was lonely, confused, and scared about his future.

When he called me later that evening, I pleaded with him to return: "I'm so sorry. I love you so much. You're my best friend! Please come back." Agreeing to try again, he came home.

In truth, Brian was my only friend in Orlando. We were solitary people who made no effort to develop a social life. Besides, I was frequently too absorbed by the work I brought home to go out at night.

Once I started paying more attention to Brian, he tried harder to build his business and was soon hired by a California production company to market a syndicated news insert. He also was renting out his camera equipment. Brian's financial situation improved. So did our marriage.

And my ceaseless efforts at work to expose and hound swindlers were rapidly earning the respect of viewers. In late 1982, the TV station offered me a two-year contract that bumped my salary to thirty thousand dollars. All of a sudden I realized that the small steps I was taking to get back on my feet were paying off. But, oddly, this did not awaken any joy in me because I was still emotionally comatose. In therapy I was working equally hard to investigate my intractable sadness and to feel worthy apart from my job.

Still, by having my own professional successes, I began to forgive my father. Why carry around my childhood forever? Besides, were it not for his faith in me, I might have remained mired in the quicksand of depression.

In January 1983, my parents came for a weekend visit and I noticed that my father looked unusually pale and almost skeletal. His voice was so faint that he could barely finish a sentence and he had constant coughing spasms. As always he didn't complain, but I knew something was wrong.

I was right to be worried. A few weeks later, he went to a doctor to find out why he had the persistent cough. An X ray showed a spot on his chest wall. From knowledge I had acquired from doing a cancer series in Dallas, I knew it was lung cancer and that it was fatal. When a biopsy confirmed a malignancy, I threw out my cigarettes and never smoked again.

Over the next few months I flew to New York every two weeks to see my father. In October, when he was hospitalized and the oncologist determined he was too weak for another chemotherapy treatment, I spent every weekend with him.

We did a lot of talking in the hospital during the last week of his life and I came to know and cherish the softer, gentler side of my father. He never mentioned the excruciating pain and discomfort he must have felt and his ferocious will to live was remarkable.

On October 24, 1983, my father died. He was cremated in a private family ceremony and a few weeks later a thousand people, including clients and business associates, came to a memorial service to honor him. I heard wonderful and funny stories about his legal brilliance, decency, and unfailing consideration for others.

It was so ironic that my failed suicide made it possible for me to resolve the conflicts with my father before he became ill. Nothing was left unsaid when he died. There were no loose ends to unravel my life again.

By April 1983, Brian and I were able to afford to rent a better house and, along with Churchill and his new sister, Beijing, we moved to a private community called The Springs. Surrounded by a panoply of trees—oaks, firs, pines, and palms—it was the perfect backdrop for a runner.

My childhood haven had been the branches of a mighty oak in our backyard. The trees all over the property were, in some way, a foundation for knowledge: solid, immutable, unassailable like the values that informed our family life. We were taught to tell the truth, to treat people with fairness and decency, and to act with integrity. If we saw an injustice and had the power to stop it, we had a responsibility to do so.

My addiction to running replaced my addiction to cigarettes and became an evening ritual. But during this time, I also began to have a problem with a weakness in my left leg. Two orthopedists diagnosed "runner's knee" and prescribed anti-inflammatory drugs.

In 1986, three years and many prescriptions and foot braces later, a neurologist would tell me my leg problem was caused by a disease of the central nervous system called multiple sclerosis.

Although I had MS symptoms back in 1976, the illness stayed dormant until 1983. I believe the stress of my father's illness and death may have activated it.

In early 1984, Brian's syndication contract ended and he sold his camera equipment to reimburse my father's estate for the previous loan. Although he wanted to work again as a television news director, the local stations in Orlando had a policy of not hiring spouses of reporters at either the same or competing newsrooms. Brian's "macho" pride prevented him from talking about his frustrating and fruitless job search or asking for my help. When he stopped trying, I began to shut him out and our relationship faltered once again. We were so out of sync that I told Brian I wanted to separate.

Devastated, he promised to look for work and begged me to reconsider. I did and soon after that Brian was hired as a producer for CNN in Atlanta. But neither of us could get used to the long-distance marriage so Brian quit after two months.

Forced to change his career, Brian combined his management skills with his devotion to golf and became a marketing director in the golf industry. Now that he was working full-time and feeling better about himself, our marriage became more stable. In 1985, we made Orlando our permanent residence and bought a small house in The Springs.

Until then I had never owned property because I considered every place I moved for work a temporary situation. From my peripatetic travels, I discovered that I could not live anywhere that was cold, crowded, noisy, or dirty. For me bigger is not better; it is only bigger.

During the same year, my contract expired and a dispute in negotiating a new agreement almost ended my revitalized career. Station management refused to give me the tools I needed to do my job well: a second phone line, a full-time assistant to handle the huge volume of calls and letters from consumers, and a cameraman assigned to the beat.

And after a few irate car dealers threatened to cancel advertising as punishment for my sting operation exposing auto repair rip-offs, the station manager wanted to muzzle my investigations. He refused to extend a clause in my expiring contract that allowed me to quit if my Action Reporter beat were eliminated.

When I balked at signing without this protection and said I preferred to work without a contract and raise, the manager and the then news director teamed up to bully me. Using the noncompete clause in my expiring contract as a weapon, they told me if I didn't sign the contract I couldn't work for the station. And if I didn't work there, I would be barred from working as a TV reporter in Central Florida for one year. I didn't want to move in order to work because Orlando was now my home.

I was not aware of my popularity in the community and only later did I learn that, according to the station's research, I was now the most credible and respected reporter in Central Florida. So while the station wanted to shut my big consumer advocate mouth, it did not want me working for the competition. When I refused to sign what I believed to be an untenable contract, the station manager fired me.

Brian, acting as my agent, then made an overture to my present employer, WCPX-TV (Channel 6). There was no argument. General Manager Mike Schweitzer gave me everything I requested: my own consumer unit with a private office, three phone lines and a full-time assistant, and cameraman R. C. Lee, who was now working for Channel 6. In addition, my salary was doubled to sixty-four thousand dollars.

On March 27, 1985, I went on the air as the Action 6 Reporter for my new employer, WCPX-TV. On March 28, I was off the air because my former employer had filed suit to enjoin me from working as a television reporter.

The day after the court hearing, I waited in my office for my lawyer to call with the judge's decision. The news director knocked on my door. "Brian is on the phone," he said. "You can use my office."

Smiling confidently at the *Orlando Sentinel* reporter and photographer who were there to record my reaction to the verdict, I excused myself. Passing through the newsroom, silenced by the unfolding drama, I felt as if I were walking a gauntlet.

I picked up the phone: "Brian?"

"I'm sorry, honey, we lost. You're off the air for a year."

I could not believe it! Like the consumers who call me, I thought, *How could this happen? It's not fair! It's not right!* But there was no one to speak on my behalf, to say to Channel 9: "Stop it. You can't treat people this way."

I fought off thoughts that I had deceived myself into believing I was okay. Maybe I had been running so fast, almost rushing past my life, that I had failed to notice someone had stuck a foot out to trip me. It was a hard fall.

I returned to my office and tried to appear nonchalant about my worst defeat in five years when I told the *Sentinel* reporter about the judge's decision.

But I couldn't fake it. I fell into a chair, wrapped my hands around my eyes, and wept. The next day my grief was displayed on the newspaper's front page.

I was inconsolable for days. Brian spent hours holding me: "I love you. Churchill and Beijing love you. You'll get past this. You'll be back stronger than ever! And while you wait out the year, you can work for WCPX as a producer and Mike Schweitzer is arranging for you to do on-air Action Reports for WDBO radio."

It was not enough. I still felt defeated.

But a few months later, it was Channel 9's turn to lose. When I learned the owners were trying to sell the station, I filed an EEOC complaint citing wage disparities between men and women. Because this could delay the sale, Channel 9 made a deal to end our dispute. I was back on the air.

As it turned out, this painful experience was fortuitous. The highly favorable publicity I received during the dispute increased my recognition. But much more important, I was no longer working for a station that would have discarded me when the MS became a problem.

I had survived. My marriage was flourishing; my career was still intact; my psychiatrist had released me from therapy. I was going to make it, after all. I felt promise in my life.

Part II

Any idiot can face a crisis.
It's this day-to-day living
that wears you out.
                    —Anton Chekhov

CHAPTER 6

After the Diagnosis: Moving On

Summer/Fall 1986

It's 5 A.M., time to get up and play "Beat the MS." Despite my fatigue and pain in the left hip, I get out of bed, pick up my leg weights, and go to the living room.

This is not fair! I never did any physical exercise until I was thirty years old. At thirty-eight, I stopped smoking and got hooked on running. Then, five months ago, just after turning forty-one, I learned I was stumbling when I ran because of multiple sclerosis and had to quit.

The day after the diagnosis, I started working with a physical therapist who assured me that, within six months, I'd have enough strength to use the Nautilus machines and might eventually run again.

The morning exercise regimen he designed for me seems to be paying off. In July, when I saw Dr. Scheinberg, my disability score was 2.5, down a half a point, on a scale of 0 to 10, the latter being the worst. I'm convinced when it drops to 0, I'll be able to run again.

At Scheinberg's insistence, I see him every three months so he can monitor how I am doing on the Imuran, the immunosuppressant he prescribed to slow the MS progression. Additionally, he reviews the results of my monthly blood tests. I feel Scheinberg is truly on the case and I appreciate his vigilance. No question about it, he is rooting for me to run again.

On the floor with a ten-pound weight around my left ankle, I begin the count: *Up—hold—down*, twenty times as my physical therapist has instructed. Churchill and Beijing, happy to be at eye level, are joyfully running around and over me.

As I work the leg, I remind Churchill to watch my August junk-of-the-month story at six. This is a light, albeit not a lightweight, way to warn naive consumers about tawdry mail-order merchandise and boiler room bums tricking people into buying overpriced products in return for worthless prizes.

The schemes are endless: the four-dollar emerald that is just a green speck worth less than the stamp used to send in the order; the incredible night-driving, vision-enhancing glasses that kill your vision; the lottery scheme promoted by the world-renowned Madame Daudet, who, in reality, is Benny Buxton of New Jersey; and the inflatable motorboat—with a one-hundred-dollar redemption fee—that cruises at a top speed of one mile an hour and sinks with more than fifty pounds in it.

A few months ago, I thought it would be interesting if Churchill ordered a junky TV dish satellite (in reality, a cheap TV antenna). He is now on every mail-order sucker list and my mailbox is littered daily with solicitations for "Mr. Churchill." He's received offers to buy an adjustable bed; a cologne guaranteed to make him irresistible to women; and bikini underwear. There are also *"Urgent!"* cards about prizes Churchill has won, including three notifications that he is a verified first-round cash prize winner in a one-hundred-thousand-dollar sweepstakes.

One of the more egregious come-ons is the letter Churchill received this month from Reverend Ike. It is this month's junk. On the letterhead, there is a photo of a smiling Reverend Ike, who writes that he is so "happy, happy, happy" as he prays for my dog to come into a large sum of money.

Enclosed is play money, a fake one-thousand-dollar bill. Churchill is supposed to sleep on a corner of the fake money overnight and then send it back with twenty dollars. Reverend Ike will then let Churchill know if the Lord shows any interest in making him rich.

Ten—hold—eleven . . . The leg feels like a dead weight, upsetting me almost as much as Reverend Ike's scheme. Fortunately, Churchill doesn't have twenty dollars, but what about others who received the same letter: the infirm or elderly who live on fixed incomes? The money they send Reverend Ike could be used to buy food or medicine.

Nineteen . . . *twenty* . . . "That's it, guys," I tell Churchill and Beijing. "I have to get ready for work." Before I leave for the station, I wake Brian, kiss him good-bye, and tell him I'll see him at the beach tonight.

We bought a weekend condominium in New Smyrna Beach, about an hour's drive from Orlando, only two weeks before the MS diagnosis. Having bought a house in The Springs last year, 1985, we use the beach place weekends only. But I don't regret the purchase because this is not a fatal disease that demands we suddenly start divesting ourselves of possessions and, besides, Brian and I find weekends at the beach restorative.

When I bound into my office at 7 A.M., my assistant, Gloria Roberson, is waiting for me. Before this job, she was a secretary for the news director at my former station. When she was fired for insubordination, I rescued her from the unemployment line.

Although minor criticism causes Gloria to weep and brings out the whine in her voice, it's more than offset by her hard work, loyalty, and efficiency.

Gloria has a hard time keeping up the pace as I head for the lounge to get coffee. She recommends, "You'd better slow down and limp or no one will believe you have multiple sclerosis."

I stop myself from saying, "That's okay, because neither do I." Instead, I explain that others cannot see what I feel: numb legs and feet, extreme fatigue, and the frequent need to urinate.

Bewildered, Gloria blurts out, "But you look so healthy."

"I am healthy!" I say forcefully. "MS is a neurological condition, not a fatal illness." I also attribute my fit appearance to my exercise regimen. In addition to the morning leg raises, I walk four miles every night on my treadmill. I bought this equipment with money I saved after I stopped smoking three years ago.

"When R.C. comes in, tell him we have to leave by ten," I instruct Gloria. R. C. Lee, my cameraman on the slum landlord series, is another casualty of my former station. When he was fired because the news director thought he had a bad attitude, I helped him get this job with my present employer.

Although some see R.C. as a large black man with a wary, antagonistic look, I know he is a kind, gentle, and thoroughly decent man.

I have just completed an investigation of Stephen Rics, the owner of an airline company that has no planes. He is running employment ads for his planeless airlines and has collected thousands of dollars in application fees from out-of-work pilots and flight attendants. Before he takes thousands more from them for training, I plan to expose his scheme next week.

He has refused to do an on-camera interview and has lied repeatedly when returning my calls. Because I want to show his face when I air the report, R.C. and I are making an unannounced visit to his office.

It's 8 A.M., two hours before I have to leave. I spend the time reviewing several stories in progress and discussing future possibilities with Gloria, as well as giving her instructions about work that needs to be completed today. I also ask her to check with the FAA and airport to reconfirm Stephen's failure to acquire any planes or apply for required licenses. When she goes back to the newsroom, I return about a dozen phone calls and read the letters she left on my desk.

One from a legal services attorney gets my attention. It says, in effect, the law couldn't help a seventy-six-year-old woman who was duped into buying a car she couldn't afford.

The woman had gone to an auto dealer after seeing his ad for a fifty-five-hundred-dollar red car. She was sold a red car that cost fourteen thousand dollars and had no air conditioning or power steering. However, it did have pinstripes on the doors, a sunroof, and an elaborate cassette system with four stereo speakers.

When she got home she realized it was not the red car advertised and most of her income, a monthly Social Security check, would be depleted by the car payments. She brought the car back to the salesman, who said, "Tough. It's your car. You signed the contract."

This salesman was disgusting, a real pig. But it was a legal transaction. I call the victim to get more information and set up an interview. "I don't want to be on television," she says in a trembling voice. "I'm too embarrassed and my friends will find out how stupid I was."

As a general practice, I don't work on a story if the victim refuses to talk on camera. But I can't disregard this woman's pain, and putting her face on television would only strip away more of her dignity. I tell her that I will do my best to help.

I immediately call the owner of the dealership. "He's not available," says his secretary. I leave a message.

It's time to leave for my unscheduled appointment with the airline mogul. R.C.'s camera is on when we get to Stephen Rics's office on the third floor of a small commercial building located near the airport. The only person I see is a very heavy woman who announces herself as the secretary and says her boss will be in at noon.

"Do you know where Stephen parks his airplanes?" I ask.

"You'll have to ask him."

"Thanks for all your help. We'll be back."

I don't want Stephen to see our news car when he arrives, so R.C. and I decide to check on the whereabouts of another con man, also in the transportation industry. This one owns a limousine service without limousines and sells a credit card that will pay for rides in the limousines he doesn't have. As R.C. and I walk into this entrepreneur's office, he is on his way out.

"Where are your limousines?" I ask.

"Every time I turn around, you're standing there!" he screams. "Leave me alone!"

As he gets into a jalopy, I tell him, "I'll leave you alone when you stop coming up with schemes to cheat people."

Then, it's back to Stephen's office. The fat woman opens the door when I knock and then slams it shut.

When I return to the office, I do more checking on Stephen's past and learn this is a repeat performance—that he was arrested after pulling the same phony airline scam a few years earlier in California. By next week, I have his mug shot in hand, and the day after my report airs, Stephen Rics leaves town.

I get an award for the investigation. Stephen Rics, arrested and extradited to Florida, is given a two-year jail sentence for grand theft and ordered to make restitution to victims.

There's no message from the auto dealer so I make another call. This time, he is away from his desk. I leave another message.

R.C. shows me the edited junk-of-the-month story about Reverend Ike. In the final shot, Churchill is barking at the picture of the smiling reverend.

I'm on the air at six:

> I interviewed Reverend Ike ten years ago in New York City. He preaches "green power." He sat in a red velvet gold leaf chair and sipped something from a twenty-four-karat gold goblet.
>
> When the interview ended, Reverend Ike put on his full-length chinchilla coat and left in his chauffeur-driven Rolls-Royce. I'll bet he didn't get that by sleeping on paper money . . .
>
> Postal inspectors tell me they've received a large number of complaints about Reverend Ike's letter and they're investigating.
>
> This makes Churchill so *happy, happy, happy*. I'll let you know.

After the newscast, I call the car dealer again and am told he has left for the day. Because I don't want the seventy-six-year-old woman to worry all weekend about the car she can't afford, I call the dealer at home. I relate the story about his customer's fourteen-thousand-dollar red car.

"So?" he grouses. "What do you expect me to do?"

"The right thing," I say. "What would you do if this were your mother?"

He must care about his mom because he pauses and then says softly, "I'm sorry. Ask her to meet me at my office tomorrow. I'll cancel the contract and make sure she gets the car she wants. My salesman's behavior is unacceptable. He will be fired."

I believe he thinks an Action 6 report about this car sale is also unacceptable. Clearly, he doesn't want me nosing around his dealership. It disturbs me that the threat of publicity is too often the only way to make some business owners act honorably.

I call the woman back to tell her about my discussion with the car dealer. She says I will always be in her prayers. Without using names, I later tell her story in a radio report. I hope that senior citizens will realize they should not sign contracts they don't read or don't understand and that it might be helpful to ask a friend or relative to accompany them when they're shopping for a car or other expensive merchandise.

On the drive to the beach, I think about the past week and how much I love my job. I wonder if MS will eventually restrict my activities. But it is only a fugitive thought.

The next day, I take a predawn walk on the beach. When I finish, I relax at the water's edge to watch the sun come up, and converse with the baby seagulls.

"So what's new, Myrtle?"

"How's your sister, Seymour?"

"Are you losing weight, Thelma?"

I look at the horizon of ocean, beyond which lie countries I want to explore while I am still able-bodied. I decide to spend my next vacation in Russia.

Brian joins me on the beach after his morning golf game. I have never understood his addiction to hitting a tiny ball that looks as if it were pitted with acne scars. Besides, I'm uncomfortable with the language of golf: "What's your handicap?"

In the early afternoon, we go for a drive. Although the sun burns in the sky and the heat is withering, Brian wants to remove the top on his Corvette. "Please leave it on," I ask him. "It's too hot."

Irritated, he says, "You never want to do anything. You don't appreciate nature." I am too faint to answer his reproach and think I might have a greater adversary for the moment—MS.

As we drive, I feel suffocated by the heat and, minutes later, when we stop for ice cream, I am unable to lift my legs. I cannot even swivel them. Brian has to pick me up and carry me into the store.

"What happened?" he asks.

"I think it's the MS," I mutter. "Dr. Scheinberg said something about staying out of the heat."

Brian looks alarmed: "Oh, my God, I'm so sorry." He rushes outside to put the top back on his car.

It turns out to be unnecessary, after all, because twenty minutes later, I feel normal again. The MS is like a phantom, vanishing as quickly as it appears.

But Brian refuses to pretend that this is an isolated MS attack. When we get in the car, he puts his hand on my arm, as if to hold me to a thought. "Ellen," he says, "I'm worried. This could happen in a parking lot when you're too far away to get help."

"It won't," I assure him. "It's not a problem."

He persists. "We should get a handicapped parking sticker for you."

"For what? I can't believe we're having this discussion."

"You never want to discuss the MS," Brian accuses. "I'm afraid to even mention it to you. That's why I ignore it."

What he says is true. Because I don't make a big deal out of it, neither does he. My position is that thinking you have MS makes it real. Even the mention, the mere articulation of the two letters, MS, the naming of the name, gives it power.

Brian makes another appeal: "If you get the sticker you don't have to use it. We'll lock it away in the glove compartment."

I explain that if you start going out and doing things like getting a handicapped parking sticker, it could be a jinx. And then capitulating to it could make you lazy when you're perfectly capable of walking long distances.

"The sticker is an MS label," I say. "Why don't we just take a megaphone to a huge parking lot and make a public announcement about my MS?"

Brian is not amused: "I disagree. At least think about it."

"Okay," I relent, "but I'll have to limp when I get out of the car." Actually, I intend to lock it away in the glove compartment like an unused emergency candle in a utility closet.

Brian is still upset so I tell him about the voice I heard a few nights ago when I was sleeping. It wasn't a dream. Someone said, "Don't worry, Ellen, you'll be fine." I didn't know why the voice was telling me this, because I *am* fine.

Dr. Scheinberg also thinks I'll be fine. At least that's what he tells me when I see him in October. "Your condition is stable," he says. "The Imuran is working."

Still, the exam itself is strange. It begins with a lot of weird questions, about a hundred in all, about every possible body function, from cognition to urination. The inquisitor is Scheinberg's associate, Dr. Charles Smith. With his furry crew cut and shiny face that almost looks buffed, he reminds me of an earnest schoolboy.

He probes: "Are you having any sexual problems?"

"No," I reply and think that's because I am not having sex. Numbness and fatigue have flattened my desire.

"Has your handwriting changed?"

"No, it's still lousy."

During this visit I find it easy to walk heel to toe down a corridor. "That's interesting," Dr. Smith remarks. "Most MS patients can't do that." I am unaware of the significance of my achievement and years later, when I think back on this session, I, the relentless reporter, am astonished by my lack of curiosity about the questions. I guess acknowledging them would have legitimized the MS.

When I leave, I tell my older sister, Karen, who is with me, that I felt like a contestant on the TV game show "Jeopardy."

"The category is chronic illness," I explain. "Your sex life vanishes. Your handwriting is a mess. You get up several times during the night to urinate . . ."

"WHAT IS MS?"

Reluctantly, Karen joins in the game. "Your mother, brothers, and sisters keep staring at you. They repeatedly ask how you feel."

"WHAT IS THE FAMILY OF SOMEONE WITH MS?" I answer.

The driver stops to let Karen off at her office and we say good-bye. On the ride to the airport, I sit back against the seat and close my eyes. Suddenly, I think about my father's journal; in it were unusual words and passages from books as well as personal thoughts. He told me about the journal a few days before he died. I now realize it was no accident that he wanted me to have his journal.

I think I know how he felt when he wrote: "Death is the most solitary of all human experiences."

I know he would understand the final "Jeopardy" question: "A deep personal pain you can't share with anyone."

"WHAT ELLEN FEELS ABOUT THE UNCERTAINTY OF MS?"

CHAPTER 7

It's Gone—
It's Back—
It's Gone?

1987–1988

I wake one morning in late August 1987 with a migraine. Aspirin doesn't help, and after two days I realize the pain is not a headache. It's emanating from my eyes. On the off-chance that it's MS-related, I call Dr. Scheinberg. "It sounds like optic neuritis," he tells me. "It's a common MS problem."

Optic neuritis, inflammation of the optic nerve, is often the first sign of MS. An attack can last anywhere from a few days to several months. The resulting loss of myelin delays the signal from the brain to the eye. It can result in temporary or permanent blindness.

Scheinberg gives me two options: a short course of steroids to lessen the severity and duration of the attack, or Tylenol. I opt for the latter because, in this case, steroids are only palliative. I also don't believe the benefits outweigh the potential risks of organ damage and such unpleasant side effects as weight gain, bloating, and acne. I am already taking two potent medicines: the immunosuppressant Imuran and Cylert to reduce MS fatigue.

The attack, which lasts three weeks, leaves me with dim vision. Colors look faded and objects lack definition, as if lighted by only a twenty-five-watt bulb. I ask Scheinberg if and when my vision will return to normal.

"In general, MS symptoms become permanent deficits," he explains, "if they last more than eight months."

His response sounds like the guess on a difficult multiple-choice question that offers no ideal responses. But MS defies a precise answer. It is not an either/or or life-or-death illness. There is no resolution.

As a reporter, I am accustomed to answers and completion. My stories have a beginning, a middle, and an end. MS, on the other hand, is a never-ending middle. And it is a disease of unpleasant surprises, such as waking up in the morning with numb feet, contracted toes, vertigo, or diminished vision. I never know if it will be all, some, or none of the above.

Why didn't Scheinberg warn me about optic neuritis? What else isn't he telling me? He may think that if I have too much information, I'll anticipate problems that may or may not happen. Above all, he wants me to put the MS aside and go on with my life.

The summer of 1987 is my first bad MS spell. First, the optic neuritis; then I drop everything I pick up and one morning while dressing for work I can't button my blouse. After struggling for fifteen minutes, I wake Brian and at the edge of tears say, "I'm sorry, but my fingers are numb. I can't get the buttons through the holes." As Brian fastens my blouse, I feel panicky, pleading, "I hope this won't be a problem every day."

"Don't worry," he soothes. "It won't be a problem because I'll just do the buttons for you."

But I don't want Brian to become my parent, dressing me like a little girl for school. It's hard enough to contend with the almost daily calls from my family. "Are you sure you're feeling okay?" they ask, as if there's something really wrong with me. While I appreciate their concern, I do not want to be reminded that I have MS.

Exercise is making me physically stronger, helping me control MS symptoms and maintain muscle memory. With MS, if you stop making a movement, the body will forget how it is done. Functions lost are rarely recoverable.

It takes six months of daily leg lifts with weights at home before I am strong enough to use the Nautilus equipment at the gym. Beginning at 6 A.M., three days a week, I press fifty pounds on the pectoral machine, push one hundred pounds on the leg press, and do squats with one hundred and twenty pounds around my waist. For trunk balance, crucial to staying on my feet, I stand on one foot at a time for five minutes with my eyes closed.

Every evening at home I walk two miles in twenty minutes on my treadmill and go up and down the stairs three times without holding on to the banister. On weekends, in a wet vest that keeps me buoyant, I jog for an hour in a swimming pool.

Every movement is a victory. And there is a cosmetic bonus as well. I look great, my cellulite is gone, and I'm all muscle.

In August, I begin an investigation that demands extra legwork. While I should wait until the cool weather returns in the fall, this story is too important for me to delay. It involves employees of a pest control company who prey on lonely old women with limited resources.

The elderly are particularly vulnerable because their generation trusted people to behave honorably. I often think of myself as their defender. For many of them, retired and living on fixed incomes, there is no chance, when swindled, to make up their losses. Too proud to ask their children to bail them out, they feel beaten—too weakened by age to fight back and without resources to hire a lawyer. And because memory loss can often make them poor witnesses, prosecutors may have difficulty proving their allegations in court.

Dorothy, age eighty-five, did not know she was a victim until her grandson, Eric, arrived from New Jersey to take her home from the hospital following hip surgery. While organizing her bank statements, he noticed numerous canceled checks made out to a Fred

Chanconi. A five-hundred-and-sixty-dollar monthly Social Security check and forty thousand dollars left by her husband when he died was all the income Dorothy had for the rest of her life and Eric was alarmed when he saw that her savings account had been reduced by ten thousand dollars. This was the exact amount Dorothy had paid Fred over a ten-month period.

When Dorothy defended Fred as a good friend who was just protecting her home, Eric called the local sheriff's fraud division. An officer told him the fleecing of his grandmother was a civil matter and recommended he call me at the television station. Maybe the publicity would induce the owner of the company to return Dorothy's ten thousand dollars.

After Eric told me what had happened to his grandmother, I asked an independent building inspector to look at Dorothy's trailer. His finding: she was cheated. In the first place, the work was unwarranted and in addition it was sloppy and incomplete.

This story resonates for me in a personal way. I think of my Nanny, my maternal grandmother, who died ten years ago. To me, she was inviolate territory, I loved her immensely, and I feel Eric's rage and sorrow over the violation of his own grandmother. I set up an interview with Dorothy and suggest that Eric file complaints with both the State Entomologist and the State Attorney's Economic Crime Unit.

When R.C. and I arrive at Dorothy's trailer around noon, the temperature is 100 degrees and climbing. Vapor rises from grease spots under Dorothy's beat-up old car. Caught in the dizzying shimmer of the day's heat, I feel momentarily deprived of air to breathe.

There is little relief inside her trailer, where a fan just circulates the hot air. Dorothy sits in a wheelchair at a small vinyl table. She is wearing a dark brown dress as threadbare as her self-esteem and bank account. Her deeply creased face is a sculpture of confusion and worry.

Dorothy tells me she just wanted to protect her home, something her husband used to do. He died two years ago and shortly thereafter Fred Chanconi knocked on her door. This thoroughly disgusting man even brought his laundry for Dorothy to wash each week while he ate food she prepared for him.

"So you were a little lonely?" I probe, gently.

"Yes," she sighs, "very lonely. And I trusted Fred when he said I needed the work." When the interview is over, I promise Dorothy I'll do my best to get her money back.

By the time I arrive at the TV station, I feel incredibly weak, the heat having depleted my strength. Holding on to the wall, I stagger down the hallway to the bathroom. A reporter whizzes by and calls out, "What's the matter, Ellen? Someone beat you up?"

By now this is a running joke around the office. It is intended as a sort of tribute to my fighting spirit, the way I confront the crooks. But at this moment I'm neither flattered nor amused; I am, simply, wilted.

On my way back to the newsroom, I am met by Mike Schweitzer, general manager of the station. "Hi, Ellen," he greets me, "how are you?"

A compact, efficient man, with tiny teeth that look like Chiclets, he speaks in an unemotional, kinetic rat-a-tat style that belies his gentle nature.

I try to focus on his Chiclet teeth as a way of distracting myself from the frustration and grief over the MS. It doesn't work. Suddenly, I am weeping and I think I may never be able to stop.

Mike, unfailingly decent and considerate, puts his arm around my shoulder: "What's wrong?"

"I've done everything possible to beat the MS," I plead with him as much as with myself. "But it's winning."

"Ellen," he reassures, "whatever you need we'll do. We'll make any accommodations you need."

But I do not want Mike to think of me as an invalid. I will continue to get all my work done. And besides, once summer ends, I tell Mike, the MS will give me a break.

I limp back to my office to write Dorothy's script and to call Joe Pate, the owner of the pest control company, to get his side of the story. Pleading innocence, he tries emotional blackmail, saying, "If you go on the air with these lies, my daughter, an A student, will be too humiliated to go to school."

"What about Dorothy's humiliation?" I counter. "Her checks are bouncing at stores because Fred took ten thousand dollars from her." Pate hangs up on me.

At six o'clock I am on the air with Dorothy's story:

> This story involves a man named Fred Chanconi, vice president of Pate's Exterminating and Home Repair Service of Central Florida.
>
> Dorothy, an eighty-five-year-old widow, paid Fred thousands of dollars for overpriced work she didn't need, couldn't afford, and, in part, was not even performed.
>
> Dorothy has put her home up for sale. She can no longer afford to live there. Fred Chanconi and Joe Pate would only answer my questions by phone. They insist that Fred did not take advantage of Dorothy and all the work was necessary.
>
> Dorothy says, after I called Fred, he called her and said he was getting a lawyer to sue her and then added, "I'm going to give you the biggest heart attack and it will kill you."
>
> Dorothy is very frightened. Fred denies he threatened her. I'll have more on Fred Chanconi.

My phone starts ringing as soon as I get off the air. Three elderly women tell me that Fred and his associates knocked on the door, and after befriending them, crawled underneath their houses to inspect for bugs. Twenty minutes later these parasites returned with a jar of sawdust filled with black specks. They claimed these were feces left by termites and told their victims that their homes would collapse unless support jacks were put under the foundation and insecticide was sprayed weekly to kill termites, carpenter ants, and beetles.

If a victim refused to sign a contract for the useless services, Fred and his cohorts would threaten to report her to the Health Department as a public nuisance. So either out of loneliness or terror or both, the women capitulated, paying thousands of dollars for exterminating and home repairs they didn't need and couldn't afford. I start a file for each victim.

As a result of my report, the State Attorney's office threatens to file grand theft and fraud charges against Fred and the pest control company. The owner, Joe Pate, immediately returns Dorothy's money. No charges are filed. However, I don't end my investigation. For me, Dorothy's story is just a warm-up.

In September there is an article in the papers about a young woman named Kathy Stilwell. In her mid-twenties she was a baseball champion and physical education teacher before MS sidelined her.

I call her and Kathy invites me to her home for dinner with her and her parents. Although she is in a scooter (motorized wheelchair), Kathy still retains the muscle tone of an athlete. Her warm and intelligent eyes, trained on me, produce a steadying effect. And after a few minutes of conversation I don't see her disability. Apparently MS is not an important part of Kathy's life. I am inspired by her courage and bravery and over the next few years we become good friends.

When the cooler weather arrives in October, the MS retreats; my vision is back to normal and sensation is returning to my hands. I leave for Russia on a ten-day group tour. Brian stays behind because of work.

There will be a lot of walking so at dinner the first night in Moscow, I tell the people in my group not to be concerned if I occasionally stumble or lag behind. One of them asks in a concerned voice, "Are you sick?"

"No," I answer. "I'm not sick. I just have multiple sclerosis. It's a neurological condition."

They seem relieved and over the next ten days they are helpful, without being too solicitous or intrusive. During this trip I realize that MS is teaching me to live in the moment. It slows me down, making freeze frames of my experiences and giving them clarity and nuance.

I return to work feeling strong and peppy. On my desk are letters from more victims of Pate pest control as well as a phone message from a former employee. When I return the call, he tells me he quit out of disgust at how Fred Chanconi and his associates, whenever they need money, show up at the home of an elderly widow and charge exorbitant fees to kill nonexistent bugs. Then they go underneath the trailers, the ex-employee tells me further, smoke a few joints, and laugh about the elderly people they call "droolies." But to their faces they give them compliments and conversation and make them feel special.

Enraged by these details, I will live with this story until it is resolved. It will take me two years to stop these bums and hold them accountable for their lies, thievery, and the trail they've left of poverty and shattered lives.

During this time, R.C. and I split up. He is self-destructing from alcohol and cocaine and won't admit he has a problem. He refuses my help and his short temper, erratic camera shots, and careless editing are so disruptive that I can no longer work with him.

My cameraman is now Ken Shuba. Although we get along, I can't seem to make him understand my need to conserve energy. For example, instead of getting out of the news van to ask for directions, Ken argues that I need to do it to build strength. Because people with MS look so healthy, he mistakes immobility for laziness. Nor does he understand that with MS *point of failure* means *point of fatigue.*

However, in my case, reducing my workload just means I'm as productive as everyone else. In fact, one of the consultants at the station says she would like to clone me because I am the first reporter at work in the morning and the last one to leave.

At home, my marriage is off-track once again. Our sex life has been nonexistent for the past year and I've explained to Brian that MS causes numbness and pain. Nevertheless, he still believes, in part, that I am rejecting him.

Feeling guilty, I tell Brian that I wouldn't blame him if he slept with someone else.

"Ellen," he says, softly, "I would never do that because I know it would hurt you too much."

Truthfully, it would and I am deeply moved by his loyalty and devotion to me.

We try to go out more often and I agree to use the handicapped sticker even though it makes me uncomfortable. One night we park in a handicapped space at a restaurant. I get out of the car, hide my face inside my jacket, and make a dash for the restaurant.

A man apprehends me at the door: "Why did you park in the handicapped spot?"

"I have MS."

"Is it the truth?"

"Why would I lie about something like this?"

Suddenly, recognizing me, he shrugs and says, "Well, I believe you because I know who you are."

"You're right to question me," I say. "I hope you'll continue to make sure able-bodied people don't use these parking spots."

Brian, standing next to me, is smiling. "See, Ellen," he says, "that wasn't so bad. That man didn't believe you have MS."

In November 1987, I go public with my MS. The owner of the gym I use sponsors a walk to benefit MS. As the guest host I say a few words before the walk: "Thank you for caring so much. Your donations will make the lives of people with MS a little easier."

Suddenly I feel as if I am going to cry. I can't believe I am standing there and that I have MS.

In years to follow, the event is sponsored by WDBO, the radio station that broadcasts my consumer reports. It's renamed the Ellen MacFarlane Walk for MS. From now on I can measure my MS by the annual walk and in the process raise thousands of dollars for research. People in Orlando are enormously supportive of me but I do not want to become their poster child. Besides, I am confident the MS will disappear.

By the end of 1987, my limp is completely gone and I am feeling stronger. One Saturday morning after a two-mile walk, I shower and change for lunch with Brian's parents, who are visiting for the weekend. As we walk up a flight of stairs to the restaurant, I suddenly know the MS is gone. Over the next few days I keep testing it. But it's not there and it's not coming back. I win! MS loses! Hooray!

———

I am right about the defeat of MS. In February 1988, Dr. Scheinberg examines me and much to his amazement and delight, there are no neurological signs of MS. I am a zero on the disability scale and my slow progressive MS is reclassified as benign sensory. This is like the difference between severe arthritis in the fingers and a sprain.

"What is my prognosis?" I query Scheinberg.

"How you are five years after the onset of MS is generally how you'll be for the rest of your life."

I want to jump up and down with relief and joy, but I'll have to wait until my legs relearn this movement. Although my MS was diagnosed two years ago in 1986, onset was ten years earlier. But even if I discount this and consider 1983, when my left leg gave out while running, as the start of my MS, I still come out ahead. In fact, even using the latter date, I am already in my sixth year of MS.

It is not unusual for MS to go undiagnosed for years. The majority of patients experience their first attacks between the ages of twenty and thirty. But the MS may not be confirmed until well into their forties and fifties and then only after a detailed medical history reveals past symptoms that were too vague or transient to be pinpointed.

Since heat is so debilitating for MS, in years past it was used as a diagnostic tool. Patients would sit in very hot water for a period of time and if their movements seemed to be impaired when they got out, this pointed to MS. In more recent times the highly uncomfortable spinal tap became the definitive test. But that, too, was flawed because MS only shows up when it is active.

Doctors now rely on magnetic resonance imaging (MRI) as well as the Evoked Potential Response test, which measures the time it takes for a signal from the eyes and the ears to reach the brain, to confirm or rule out MS.

Scheinberg increases the time between examinations from three to six months but, just in case, he wants me to continue taking Imuran. I leave his office with a big smile lighting up my face.

Now that the MS has fled, I can acknowledge it and I tell my older sister, Karen, who always accompanies me on my visits to Scheinberg, that I feel as if I've been given a reprieve from a death sentence. I am getting ready to run again.

I always like being with Karen. As a lawyer who chooses public service over private practice, she was previously, among other jobs, a state senator and the state's consumer protection chief. So we have a lot to talk about and she fills me in on the underpinnings of consumer law. And from my experiences with MS, Karen is learning about fighting for quality of life.

A person of wide-ranging intelligence and voracious curiosity, Karen wants to know everything about MS. She thinks she may have mild symptoms: stumbling and an overactive bladder. This is not farfetched because MS, according to some researchers, is now believed to be genetic. It frequently afflicts more than one person in a family and more often twins. However, only one twin generally exhibits symptoms.

Karen's driver drops me off at my twin Patricia's apartment, where I am staying overnight. Immediately I call Brian to relay the good news. He is on his way home so I leave a message with his secretary: "Please tell Brian I'm a zero."

To be sure, only someone who has had a previous run-in with MS and overcome it would speak of herself this way.

I call my mother, who says, "Oh, Ellen, I'm so delighted," which mirrors the reaction of my brothers and sisters, who either call or drop by before I go out for the evening. As a belated birthday gift, Judd, the youngest, is taking Patricia and me to dinner and *M. Butterfly* on Broadway.

While I'm dressing, Brian calls and congratulates me for the zero disability score. However, he seems more cautious than celebratory. "How do you know it's gone?" he presses me.

"All I know," I insist, "is that Dr. Scheinberg classifies my MS as benign sensory and says I shouldn't have any more problems."

"How could it just simply disappear?"

"The Imuran did it. How come you're asking all these questions? Why aren't you just glad it's gone?"

"I *am* happy," Brian says, "but I worry it could come back again."

The uncertainty of MS is just as difficult for spouses as it is for patients. And Brian wants to protect me, as much as himself, from any future disappointment if the MS returns to impose on our lives again. He is not entirely wrong.

There are no guarantees with MS. It is different for everyone and, it could be said, it is also many different diseases. The only predictable factor is its unpredictability. I am now one of some 20 percent who have *benign* MS, the least intrusive. Attacks are early, infrequent, and mild; there is minimal or no disability.

About 25 percent have exacerbating/remitting MS: attacks are early, more frequent; remissions are long but less stable; and there will be some degree of disability. The 40 percent with chronic/relapsing MS have fewer remissions and disability is cumulative and moderate to severe.

The remaining 15 percent are hit with the most insidious form of MS, chronic progressive: a downhill course without remissions resulting in severe disability—paraplegia, quadriplegia, muscle weakness (with or without spasticity or contractures of skin and joints), severe incoordination, loss of bladder control and bowel function, and, in rare cases, dementia.

Although MS itself almost never causes death, secondary problems can be fatal. They include lung and urinary tract infections, severe and intractable contractions, and pressure sores that become infected.

"What a relief it is to only have benign MS," I say happily to Patricia as we leave her apartment. "It must be awful to be chronic progressive. I don't think I could handle it."

At dinner Judd, Patricia, and I celebrate the departure of MS with champagne. Judd is always great company. A lawyer, he is wonderfully articulate and witty and his legal briefs are uncommonly lively, never turgid. Sometimes, with his baby face, it is hard to accept he is all grown up.

It is a long evening because Judd is also a bon vivant. After the theater, the three of us trundle off to a private club-cum-disco for a nightcap. I have no problem getting down the stairs into the place, but I still can't dance. The MS is gone, but it has left me with some deficits: a slight, though almost imperceptible limp, loss of flexibility and strength. This doesn't bother me because I know I'll be dancing again in a few months.

The next evening, at dinner with my family at our home on Long Island, everyone says I look wonderful. We catch up on each other's lives and for the first time since the diagnosis two years ago, MS does not even figure into our conversation.

Yet it is the MS that is bringing me home again. Though I still feel as if I have to prove myself to my brothers and sisters by showing them videos of my stories, I now know they will always stick by me.

Brian's behavior sometimes feels less certain. Back in Orlando, when I try to resume a sexual life with Brian, he's unwilling. Worn out by the mercurial nature of MS with its on-again, off-again behavior, he says it will take time for him to readjust to life without MS.

But there are, happily, no adjustments to make at work where I continue to prosper. I put my ongoing pest control investigation on hold to pursue another story I've been following for two years. This one involves the owner of a new three-hundred-thousand-dollar house who sues his builder, David Kippel, and wins a ten-thousand-dollar judgment, still uncollected. Kippel closes his business, transfers all his assets to his wife's name, and refuses to pay the debt. On the phone with me, he defends his shoddy behavior with a shoddy excuse: "Oh, no one is ever satisfied. You can't expect a house to be perfect."

"There has apparently been a misunderstanding," I tell Kippel. "Your client didn't expect perfection, he only expected to get the home he paid you to build. And the court expects you to pay the ten-thousand-dollar judgment."

The Department of Professional Regulation (DPR), which polices the construction industry, is also a culprit in this case. Seven months earlier, at my suggestion, the aggrieved homeowner filed a complaint against the builder. The agency found Kippel guilty of misconduct and threatened to revoke his license if the ten-thousand-dollar judgment was not paid.

Kippel, who owns two homes and drives a thirty-thousand-dollar Mercedes, pleaded poverty and threatened to declare bankruptcy to avoid honoring the debt. Falling for his bluff, the DPR fined Kippel a paltry five hundred dollars and suspended his contractor's license for a mere thirty days. However, the suspension will be revoked once Kippel pays the fine.

When I show up at Kippel's home in Sarasota, he refuses to answer any questions. I quote him in my report on the six o'clock news:

> David Kippel tells me he doesn't care what I say about him. Okay, David, you're a creep! And the DPR should have revoked your license. I'll be meeting with the head of the DPR in Tallahassee this week. I'll let you know.

My investigation of how the Department of Professional Regulation fails to discipline contractors who cheat consumers wins a Florida Press award and inspires a new segment, "There Ought to Be a Law." In this case there should be a law requiring contractors to post a performance bond to pay debts to home owners and to ensure that work is satisfactorily completed.

Shortly after I finish skewering the DPR, I learn there is a space for me in the Jimmy Heuga program in Vail, Colorado. It is a comprehensive MS center founded by its namesake, skiing champion Jimmy Heuga. MS ended his career six years after he won the bronze medal in the slalom event at the 1964 Winter Olympics in Innsbruck.

Prior to the demise of my MS, I had applied to the center's week-long evaluation and individually designed exercise program. Although I can now move better, feel generally more comfortable, and my feet no longer seem to be attached to heavy weights, I am still unable to run. I want confirmation that the MS is not lurking around my life so, in July 1988, I begin the Heuga program.

Experts claim that 75 percent of MS patients remain ambulatory. Well, I keep asking myself, where are they? The only ones I ever see are in wheelchairs, which is pretty much the situation at the Jimmy Heuga Center.

And although MS patients are cautioned about comparing themselves with others because it is such an unpredictable, individual disease, we always do: "Hey, that person's worse than I" or "That person's doing much better. Why can't I be like that?" This is the perfect place to measure my progress at beating the MS.

In one class, when they demonstrate wheelchair exercises, I ask why I need to learn this. "Because," the instructor tells me, "someday you may need to know what to do if you are in a wheelchair." I am flabbergasted. To me, this is like taking someone to a cemetery when they have a heart condition.

There are lectures on bladder and bowel control, spasticity, massage, and stress reduction. In order to design an exercise program for my needs, physical therapists test my coordination, balance, and muscle strength. My walk is videotaped so that they can study the width of my stance and how I position my legs when they turn. They confirm that I am in great shape.

I think that I am not even close to being in as bad a condition as those who are in relatively good shape at the center. Looking at me, no one would ever know I have MS. So I am not prepared when the neurologist who examines me concludes that I have a moderate disability. On the scale of 0 to 10, my rating is 3.5.

"You don't know what you're talking about," I rage. "Dr. Scheinberg gave me a zero. You're just seeing the deficits caused by the MS I no longer have!"

A psychologist, trying to calm me down, says that I have to learn to accept the MS. I tell her that I've already gone through the acceptance process and have no intention of repeating the experience.

Besides, what do these people know? They are the same ones who ask me if I am an alcoholic when my blood tests show large red blood cells and low folic acid. I am greatly offended. Had they studied my medical records more closely, they would have known the Imuran I take causes these problems.

Nonetheless, I find that I can no longer be so cavalier about my condition. Now I am caught in my own self-deception. In my room, I sob for two days.

When I call Brian he is just mean. "Stop crying about it," he snaps. "I just can't go through this. One day you have it and the next you don't. What am I supposed to do?"

Upon my return home, I speak to Scheinberg, who diffuses the finding from the Heuga program. He says there is nothing to indicate I have deteriorated. "You're benign sensory," he explains, "which means that you still have MS but you'll be like this—no worse—the rest of your life."

I do not believe he is fooling me as a way to rescue me from disappointment. Scheinberg is a truth-teller. Besides, after the Heuga program, I don't feel any signs of the MS. I am even able to run an eighth of a mile. Because my left side is now so strong, I don't notice the increasing weakness on my right side. The reason? I am overcompensating.

When I think about my experience in the Jimmy Heuga program, I realize that I learned a great deal about MS and about myself. And Jimmy Heuga told us something that is very important. "You're not handicapped," he explained. "You're physically challenged."

I now know that everybody has something in their life that stops them short, limiting them in some way. What I have is just more visible.

Fortunately, the MS continues to stay out of my way at work. In the fall of 1988, Brian negotiates a great contract for me. Because of the heat, I will not work from June 15 to September 15 and my salary for nine months of work is one hundred and twenty-five thousand dollars. They give me a huge office on the second floor with a separate air-conditioning unit. It is only a few feet from the bathroom. The room is also wired so that I can watch my stories as they're being edited on the first floor and I hire another assistant, part-time, to help Gloria. Best of all, I gain full editorial control of my stories.

I can't believe it. I've come a long way from making lopsided ashtrays at Elmcrest. Was that only seven years ago? I feel proud about my achievements.

And Brian really came through for me yet again. It is an important victory for him as well—a reminder of his potential as a very smart and enterprising man who is also imaginative, well read, and amusing.

It's hard to be married to a woman who is a ubiquitous force in the community. Whenever we go out in public, people come up to me and tell me their problems. Mail addressed to "Ellen MacFarlane, Orlando, Florida," even reaches me.

Despite past difficulties in our marriage, I know Brian is rooting for me and, if the MS ever really gets bad, I can always count on him. Throughout, he has helped me to stay steady and focused.

That weekend Brian and I go out to dinner to celebrate my new contract. When I get up to go to the bathroom, I lose my balance and bump into another table of diners, knocking over their champagne.

The six people at the table recognize me. "Hi, Ellen," one of them says. "You must be having a good time."

"You're not going to believe this," I say, "but I'm not drunk. I have MS. Please don't tell me you're sorry. Please don't tell me I'm an inspiration. Please don't think about it. It's not important. Enjoy your evening." I send a bottle of champagne over to their table.

In truth it's not important. A year ago I would have regarded this event as an indication that I was deteriorating. But that is not the case. Despite this mishap, I am confident that the MS will not impair my future.

CHAPTER 8

Two Years to Wheelchair

1989

I t's a new year and Brian and I are looking at construction plans for a house we are building on an acre of land in The Springs. As we walk across the recently cleared lot, I stumble and grab his arm to keep from falling.

"Ellen, watch where you're going," Brian says with irritation.

He is in one of his foul moods. I placate him: "Sorry, I slipped on a rock. I'll be more careful." I dare not tell him that I'm wall-walking (putting my hands on walls for balance) at the office. Such an admission would only acknowledge that the MS is back.

However, the MS does not impede my ongoing investigation of still another building contractor from hell. This time it is a condominium with structural defects including an unsupported roof, a foundation without footers, and electrical wires that are undersized and not grounded. A county building inspector overlooked these and fifty other code violations.

Three structural engineers are telling six families still living there that they are in danger because the roof will collapse on them. Yet the county attorney insists, in his bureaucratic patois of denial and myopia, that the construction meets all county codes and, further, there is nothing in writing about the roof to indicate a safety problem.

My fury is evident on the six o'clock news:

> What does it take to get someone to look at this horrendous situation? County officials should be more concerned about the safety of people than about the county's liability because the Building Department failed to do its job properly. Somebody, please pay attention!

I'm disappointed that my stories don't help the victims. The Department of Professional Regulation investigates after my reports, condemns the condominium, forcing the owners out of their unsafe homes. Sadly, they'll have to sue for restitution.

It's bad timing that the MS kicks in now, just when I am beginning to explore the scope of shoddy construction throughout Florida and the psychological and monetary devastation unscrupulous builders cause. Unfortunately, I no longer possess the endurance to plow through the thicket of incompetent and inefficient practices of state and local agencies monitoring the building industry.

It comes as no surprise when, in 1992, Hurricane Andrew quickly disassembles and demolishes houses that passed all building inspections yet looked as though they were constructed out of papier-mâché. Consumers do not realize that the protection these government agencies claim to provide is only an illusion.

Although it is not obvious to others, MS is beginning to hobble some of my legwork in the field; I have to stop running after crooks outside because I can't keep up with them and I keep tripping over my feet. During the taping of this story, I'm unable to climb up a ladder to reach the roof or walk on the uneven grass with an engineer pointing out construction flaws. Instead, I must rely on the camera-man to get most of the video I need for the story.

While I still consider MS just a minor inconvenience, late at night when I speak truthfully to myself, I acknowledge its presence and that it's progressing. Just in case, the new house will be handicapped-accessible: double-wide halls and doors, grab bars, ramps, and a garage large enough for a van.

February 1989, construction begins. To be completed by July, the 3,300-square-foot home with 12- to 24-foot ceilings will surround a large pool and include an intercom, security, and an elaborate stereo system. There will also be a separate air-conditioned suite for me with an office, a gym, a huge two-floor walk-in closet, and a bathroom.

The builder's decorator is Marsha Temple, whose use of color and form to enhance rather than obliterate natural light and open spaces pleases me. We met when she decorated my first house and we hit it off immediately.

Marsha is also my closest friend, a warm, funny, and maternal woman about my age, who is devoted to family and friends. Her husband, Wally, is just as nice and their two children, Scott and Wendy, are all the things that parents who value their children would like them to become. Thoughtful, sensitive, bright, and productive, they exemplify the best of today's youth. This is a solid family.

I wish that I could say the same about my home life. I can't. In recent weeks Brian has been consistently angry and impatient with me. Almost anything I say sets him off, producing a testy response or, alternatively, a prolonged rage.

Anyone who watches me on television would be astounded by my meek reaction to Brian's verbal abuse. I do not understand it either. But I think I excuse it because I suspect he may only be venting his frustration about his role as second fiddle to his TV star wife in Orlando. Or he may just be retaliating for my past self-absorption. So I try not to take it personally.

But it *is* personal. Brian is my husband and I expect him to treat me with respect and affection. His hostility is so alarming that, in March, I give him an ultimatum: stop the abuse or leave. I also tell him that I am having second thoughts about committing my financial resources to pay for a new house.

Brian finally talks to me about his feelings; he is chronically depressed and anxious. He follows up on my suggestion that he see a psychiatrist, who prescribes the antidepressant Prozac. Within a few weeks the medicine works, calming Brian and making him more even-tempered and agreeable to be around.

Because the people who bought our house move in the first of July, Brian and I move into our new house, although it is not yet completed. When I see the builder's definition of my handicapped-accessible bathroom I am horrified. He puts a slanted Formica panel underneath the sink to accommodate a wheelchair. But this is not my future and I insist that it be replaced with regular drawers and cabinets.

Since my contract gives me the summer off, I plan to use this time to exercise, with the goal of increasing my strength and endurance. But that's impossible due to the constant presence of workmen. Also, Brian adds to the distractions. Almost every afternoon he brings friends and co-workers to the house and he becomes annoyed when I refuse to act as a tour guide.

I notice that he is drinking heavily despite the psychiatrist's warning not to mix alcohol with Prozac. It is making him very mean-spirited.

To relieve me, Marsha supervises the ongoing construction. Brian's daughters, Tori and Amy, here for the summer, help me unpack. Now that they're older and no longer hover, I enjoy their company.

But by late July I am exhausted and look forward to being alone when Brian takes the girls to Atlanta to visit his parents for a weekend.

Since I still practice what I believe is healthy denial of MS, I don't bring my security system panic button with me Sunday afternoon when Churchill, Beijing, and I go outside to sunbathe. It's one o'clock, 100 degrees, and 100 percent humidity without a cloud in the sky. Reclining on a lounge chair, I think a tan will make me look healthier and this may help rekindle Brian's attraction for me.

But the intense heat makes me so weak that after fifteen minutes of sun, I decide to go back into the air-conditioned house. I sit up, put my lower legs over the side of the lounge, and attempt to stand up. My knees buckle and I go down and find I don't have enough strength even to hoist myself into a sitting position.

I think of the TV commercial for an emergency help system: "I've fallen and I can't get up!"

But this isn't an advertisement: I'm flat on my back on the scorching cement.

If I can just roll myself a few feet, I think, *I'll reach the door I left open to the sundeck.*

I can't move. My system is paralyzed. *This can't be happening!* I scream inside my head. But it is and I'm helpless until Brian returns home after five o'clock, about four hours from now.

Rolling onto my stomach, I inadvertently trap my right arm under my 105-pound body. For several minutes I struggle to extricate my arm. It is to no avail. I pass out from the severe pain.

Over the next four hours, I drift in and out of consciousness. I try holding my breath so I'll die, but the pain in my arm is like a rubber band snapping me back. It's terrifying as I feel my face scraping side to side across the cement and then being stretched back so tightly that the skin peels off. And I also feel my skull open and liquid pour out.

All of a sudden, I see high block letters: L O V E.

I hear a voice in my mind: "THAT'S WHAT IT'S ABOUT!"

"*THAT'S WHAT IT'S ABOUT?*" I ask in a thought.

"YES, IT'S ALL ABOUT LOVE!"

I feel myself being turned over. The pain in my arm goes away. I open my eyes and it's is very light.

"AM I DEAD?" I ask.

From far away I hear someone call my name. It's Brian. He had forgotten his key and was calling me to open the door for him when he heard the dogs barking frantically. He had climbed over the fence and found me unconscious on the cement.

My pale, clammy face is coated with an oily liquid. Brian thinks I have cracked my skull and that I am dead.

He is greatly relieved when I move my head and whisper, "Ambulance." But, knowing my terror of hospitals, Brian picks me up, carries me inside, and puts me in the tub and fills it with ice-cold water.

Within ten minutes, I'm lucid and coherent. Two hours later my strength returns and I walk normally. The only visible signs of my four-hour trauma are a few facial scrapes, a brutal sunburn on my back and behind my legs, and a slightly swollen right arm.

The next morning, I see my internist, who is surprised that I survived such a severe heatstroke. He tells me the oily fluid on my face was secretion from sebaceous glands that opened in my skull.

However, my body does not escape permanent damage and within days I need a cane for balance. I use it in public for the first time when I meet Brian and the girls for lunch. I walk over to their table, clutching the cane, tears cascading down my face. There's nothing anyone can say to console me. My body is beginning to desert me. I can't reconcile what I think I should be able to do with what my body will permit.

But, as time passes, I realize my near-death experience has profoundly changed me; the person who fell down on the hot cement is very different from the one who woke up four hours later. As my spiritual side emerges, I become more patient, considerate, and forgiving. My boundaries expand, beginning a transformation that gives me comfort, peace, and joy and will ultimately help me get past the ensuing physical deterioration from MS. I really like the person I am becoming!

Brian also seems tempered and changed by this experience. Kinder and more thoughtful, he now talks to me rather than at me.

In August we fly to New York to see Dr. Labe Scheinberg. I really like and trust this man. This time we drop the formal "Ms." and "Dr." It's now Ellen and Labe. After an examination, Labe assures me the MS is still under control.

"What about my loss of strength?" I ask.

"I think we're dealing with the NK factor," he says with amusement in his eyes.

Alarmed, I ask if this is a new MS symptom. "No," he smiles, "it means you're a natural klutz." Then, Labe lectures me: "You're a closet jock, not superwoman, your nutrition is horrendous, your sixty-hour workweek has to stop, and you need to listen to your body. To put it in computer terms, you ran out of RAM."

Relieved that I still maintain the upper hand with MS, I return to Orlando. I speak to a group of newly diagnosed people:

> When I describe MS, I use the word crooks use to describe me. MS is a bitch!
>
> It's the toughest challenge I've ever faced. It's unpredictable, often terribly inconvenient, and sometimes very frightening.
>
> I used to believe the only limitations you have are the ones you place on yourself. I still believe this applies to my personal and professional growth, but not so physically.
>
> Aside from MS, there are limitations imposed on all of us by the aging process.
>
> Now, this doesn't mean you stop challenging the changes or decide it's all over. It simply means you incorporate them into your life, stay well informed, and take a little better care of your bodies.
>
> I deal with problems right away and move on, and I still believe, despite the MS, that I will run again.

I don't like the orthopedic, stainless steel look so I start collecting unique, antique canes to use when I return to work in September. And because I can no longer walk with heels, I build a wardrobe of unusual socks and colorful laces to dress up my sneakers. It's not that I'm embarrassed by the MS or by my awkward gait, but I don't want it to become a distraction when I interview the victims in my stories.

Seeing the cane, they often apologize for bothering me. I explain that their problems are as significant to them as MS might be to me and, besides, it doesn't stop me from running over cheats and liars.

While I was away from work during the summer, the pest control creeps I'd been pursuing for the past two years were arrested and charged with grand theft. The trials begin in September and when I follow the company owner, Joe Pate, into the courtroom, he screams, *"I hope you become a cripple!"*

I think this is preferable to being a moral cripple like this parasite. He pleads no contest to two felony charges on behalf of his corporation and the judge orders him to pay thousands of dollars in restitution to three elderly victims.

I'm on the air at six:

> Joe Pate tells me I've ruined his business and his personal life. Well, let me remind you, Joe, that the vice president of your company and your employees scared a lot of good people, taking their savings and ruining their lives.
>
> The state entomologist has just filed administrative complaints against Joe Pate and his employees.
>
> I'll let you know.

In October, the state entomologist orders Joe Pate to cease and desist all pest control operations and revokes his and his employees' pest control licenses. This company is permanently out of business.

People often ask me if I'm afraid the "Joe Pates" of Orlando will do me bodily harm. I'm not. I am angry when I find crooks like Pate and his greedy employees who think they can cheat people repeatedly and walk away with impunity.

Besides, I consider threats to be an occupational hazard. I'm sure many of the people I expose fantasize about leaving me in a pond of alligators, but I don't do stories that might result in my car blowing up when I turn on the ignition. Aside from a few raised fists, one unsuccessful attempt to shove me through a plate glass window, occasional warnings to back off "or else . . ." and a lot of four-letter words I bleep before airing, I am not threatened physically. And although I occasionally receive letters from attorneys, I have never been successfully sued.

I am really pleased about the demise of Joe Pate's business. Of all the schemes I have exposed, this is the worst, the most offensive, the most harmful.

I cannot know that I have yet to meet the cruelest crook of all.

———

At my request, Labe Scheinberg is the keynote speaker at the annual Central Florida MS meeting in late October. Before the speech, Brian and I take him to lunch, where we discuss everything but MS. Labe is a Renaissance man, conversant with the classics, contemporary literature, history, and current events. A lover of words, Labe collects dictionaries and is a prolific writer. Talking with him reminds me of my late father's enormous, wide-ranging intellect.

I do not use a cane this day and hope Labe doesn't notice my lopsided walk. But he does. Later, when we stop at my house, he asks me to walk down the hallway. He talks privately with Brian and then, with sorrow in his eyes, tells me, "I'm worried, Ellen. The Imuran is no longer working. The MS is progressing. You're now chronic progressive."

This is the worst form of MS, a rapid downhill course without remissions. Cytoxan, a very toxic immunosuppressive drug, is the only available treatment and its success has only been marginal. Although it is administered by chemotherapy, Labe wants to first try a high dosage of Cytoxan in pill form.

I'm in shock when Labe and I leave for dinner. On the way to the restaurant, he blurts out, "I'm really concerned, Ellen. I don't think your ego will permit you to sit down in a wheelchair."

He's right. "I have no intention of ever sitting down," I tell him emphatically. He says nothing.

I cannot wait for dinner to end so I can go home and cry. When I return, I ask Brian about his private conversation with Labe.

Brian tells me what I do not want to believe: "Labe says they call it two years to wheelchair."

———

A few weeks later I get the flu. My immune system is so debilitated by the Cytoxan that I am in bed for six weeks. During this period, I lose so much strength that I must now use a walker as well as a cane.

Brian, meanwhile, is frequently absent. Explaining that he doesn't want to catch my flu, he leaves early and comes home late. I have no reason to believe he's lying. But he is. In December, when I hear someone leave a message for me on Brian's answering machine, I rewind the tape. The first message is from a woman saying she'll meet Brian at eight-thirty that night.

When Brian comes home at midnight and denies he's having an affair, I play the tape for him. Trapped by the evidence, he confesses, saying he had sex with the woman a few times but it was meaningless.

I demand the truth.

"You want the truth," Brian says. "You're cold and I don't want to make love with you."

His outburst is not surprising. He continues to drink and becomes so verbally abusive I stay out of his way at home and sleep in the guest bedroom.

Later on that night, when he is sober, Brian apologizes; he is sorry he hurt me, he loves me, and maybe he needs space. I tell him to look for another place to live.

A few days later, Brian accidentally switches our respective American Express card bills and leaves his on my desk. Without looking at the name, I open the envelope and discover that since early October Brian has been engaging in meaningless sex twice a week at local motels. Of course, he can afford to do this because I pay most of the household bills.

Still, I am heartbroken and advise Brian that we need to separate until he sorts out his feelings. He disagrees, insisting the affair is just sexual and he is trying to extricate himself from it.

The stress is exacerbating the MS, and I am rapidly losing mobility and starting to fall down a lot. A friend introduces me to a Colombian woman named Vicky Medina, a deeply religious Seventh-Day Adventist, whom I hire as a full-time housekeeper. She looks after me well and over the next few years I will become very close to Vicky, her two children, and her mother. She cleans, cooks, shops, and runs errands for me. Later on her duties expand.

She is always there when I need her and through it all we laugh together. I come to love this woman with a pure and generous heart.

MS has me so scared that, in December, I decide to go to New York to see Labe Scheinberg. I am too weak to travel alone and although any one of my brothers and sisters would come to Orlando to fetch me, I don't want to impose on their busy lives. And, besides, none of them knows about my marital problems.

I am more frightened of losing body function than I am of losing Brian to another woman. As a practical matter, I ask Brian to fly with me to New York. He refuses unless we go up and back the same day.

Labe, who sees my deterioration, advises me to keep walking. He also says a promising new drug may soon be available and I'll be among the first to get it.

Brian, who already had two vodkas on the flight to New York, is not the least bit comforting. In fact, he is incredibly cruel, glaring at me all day and yelling about my not moving fast enough, taking too long to put my coat on, and stopping to use a bathroom at the airport. My sister Karen, who meets me at the airport to say hello and good-bye, is appalled by Brian's nastiness. When she tells him not to be so harsh with me, he says I'm impossible and it frustrates him.

On the return flight, I realize I am allowing both Brian and the MS to control me and I am losing myself again. I cannot count on this man whom I no longer know. Brian doesn't love me. I feel emotionally abandoned.

We arrive home at seven in the evening and minutes later Brian announces he has to go to the office to attend to an emergency. But he assures me he'll be back soon.

What a liar! I think. *He's going to see that woman.*

Enough, do something, don't just retreat! I exhort myself.

When Brian goes out the door, I go into his desk drawers to search for evidence. Buried in a box of stationery is a greeting card: "I love you . . . Some day, N." I look through Brian's Rolodex and find a listing for a Noreen.

Being a highly task-oriented person is an advantage with MS; it forces me to pursue indoor activities requiring minimal mobility. At this point, I'm not only quite a computer whiz, but also somewhat of an expert in electronic eavesdropping. During Brian's increasing absences, on the golf course and more recently in motel rooms, I have been honing my skills.

Until now it seemed unthinkable to tape another person without his or her knowledge, not only because it's illegal in Florida, but also because it is a reprehensible invasion of someone's privacy. But home alone with my MS while my husband is cheating on me, I need to make some important and swift decisions about the marriage.

In case Brian comes back soon, I close the guest bedroom door and tack a note on it. "Don't come in. I'm meditating." While I am in the process of wiring Brian's phone line into the outlet in my new sleeping quarters, he returns. I don't know I've made a mistake until Brian knocks on the door to inform me that both phone lines are dead.

Thinking quickly, I tell him there's a problem in the area and the phone company says service will be restored soon.

Brian is ignorant of my electronic expertise and has yet to realize I am as thorough an investigator at home as I am at work. So he believes my story about the dead phone lines.

Actually, I am the telephone repair service and fifteen minutes later I fix the problem. Next, I attach recording equipment, with a sixty-minute tape, to Brian's line. In the morning I remove the tape and replace it with a fresh one. The original tape is full.

It takes only fifteen minutes to get to the station so I sit in my car for forty minutes listening to the entire tape. I hear Brian complain that I'm selfish and stupid. Noreen, agreeing, tells Brian not to tolerate my abuse. While she desires an end to her twenty-year common-law marriage, she worries that her partner will refuse to give her any money. No problem, says Brian, who promises that if she gets an apartment, he'll pay the rent.

I want to scream, "How dare you?" Instead I shake with pain.

If the MS has taught me anything, it's patience, and I decide to wait a few days to think about my response. Also, I want to allay any suspicions that I am monitoring his conversations, and certainly want to keep him out of the guest bedroom, central headquarters.

When the tape ends, I get out of the car, take a few deep breaths, and hang on to my walker. Gloria, whom I recently promoted to be my producer, meets me at the door and opens it for me.

"Ellen, there are twenty people waiting for you in the lobby," she reports. "They were ripped off by a pool builder. It's a great story; they're really upset. Some of them are crying."

I have to make a choice. Their agony or mine. "Put them in the conference room," I instruct Gloria, "and tell these people I'll be there in fifteen minutes. Also, ask Kenny to set up and I'll interview them with a shotgun microphone."

I go into my office and call my lawyer and good friend, Steve Fieldman. "Hi, Brian is cheating on me," I say as soon as he gets on the phone. "Can you come here today? I want a divorce and I want to change my will." Steve promises to meet me here at noon.

In the conference room I interview the twenty victims of a pool contractor named Nathan Stern. He took one hundred and seven thousand dollars from them, dug holes in their backyards, and disappeared. They will have to pay off loans for the pools they don't have and they have liens against them from subcontractors and suppliers whom Nathan never paid.

I am so absorbed by their problem that it takes the edge off mine. That night at six, I do my first story on this deadbeat:

> Nathan Stern is disgusting. He uses the names Nathan L. and Nathan E. Stern. He has two driver's licenses and at least two Social Security numbers. He's sixty-seven, five feet seven with white hair, and he has a lot of money that belongs to homeowners he cheated. Nathan Stern is a very elusive thief. If you know where I can find him, please call me at Channel 6.

It takes me two years to find Nathan Stern in Texas, where he has a whole new career as a home improvement contractor. But by the time he is extradited back to Florida to stand trial on a scheme to defraud and on grand theft charges, I'm in New York, having surrendered to a treatment with a doctor who promises to cure my MS.

At year's end, while my lawyer is preparing divorce papers, I'm preparing for life without Brian.

Nothing, not even divorce, I tell myself, can be as devastating as MS.

Only a year ago, December 1988, my marriage was secure. The MS was gone. I finally saw the light at the end of the tunnel.

December 1989, just twelve months later, a train hits me. My marriage is over. The MS is back.

CHAPTER 9

Out of Denial

1990

On an overcast morning in March, I am entering a county courthouse annex where I will end my marriage.

My good friend Marsha, who is with me for support, gently touches my arm: "Are you okay?"

"For now I am," I answer.

She sits on a bench in the hallway to wait while my lawyer and I go into a hearing room. I have no doubts about my decision. A few days ago, Brian asked me to reconsider. "What's the hurry?" he said. "Why can't we just separate?"

"You no longer love me," I answered. "In our case a separation is like being a little pregnant."

It continues to elude Brian that this divorce is not about his sexual betrayal but, rather, his deception and cruelty. Given every opportunity to tell the truth, he lied. I am finished making restitution to him for helping with my career. I owe him nothing. Further, my body cannot afford any more stress.

In the hearing room, after a few preliminary questions, the officer asks, "Why do you want a divorce?"

Following the instructions from my attorney, I answer, "There are irreconcilable differences."

In less than fifteen minutes the divorce is granted; it will become final within four weeks. If only it were as easy to end the MS.

As part of our agreement I turn over my share of the New Smyrna Beach condominium to Brian. I get the house because I paid for it.

So as not to confuse TV viewers I will still be known as Ellen Mac-Farlane on the air. But I plan to phase it out and ultimately to use only Burstein.

When my lawyer and I exit the hearing room, Marsha jumps up to greet me. "Don't worry," I preempt her. "I'm okay."

But, in truth, I don't know how I feel. I am just relieved it's over. I'm taking the day off from work and we're going out to lunch.

As we get into Marsha's car in front of the courthouse, she observes, "You seem to be handling this well."

"Look, this is only another change in my life," I respond. "I'll move past it the way I do with MS."

But I am not yet able to move beyond my rage at Brian's indecency. "It's too early for lunch," I tell Marsha. "First, let's get her!"

She grins: "Let's go." We head for the parking lot of the office where Noreen, Brian's girlfriend, works as a receptionist for a medical laboratory.

During the drive, we hatch several retaliatory plots: putting hair remover in Brian's shampoo bottle to turn him into a bald philanderer; calling utility companies to cancel Noreen's electricity, water, and telephone service; and writing a personal ad for a singles magazine that says "SWF (Stupid White Female) wants to meet WMM (White Married Man), preferably with a wife in the TV news business."

We are in stitches, laughter keeping my sadness at bay. Eventually we settle on pouring garlic and fish oil down the narrow crack in the hood of her car. Once it gets in the engine, there is no way to remove it: "Turn on the engine, turn on the odor." We stop at Marsha's house to mix the ingredients before heading for the parking lot.

We're like two soldiers on a reconnaissance mission. We do not want anyone to interrupt our campaign so Marsha patrols the parking lot while I sit in the car using binoculars to scan the area.

Twenty minutes later, when Marsha signals the coast is clear and starts walking back to the car, I begin to think this is not a healthy thing for me to do. Not only is it out of character for me to behave vindictively, but to do so would also demean and violate the kind of person I am. If I allow Brian's betrayal to paralyze me with rage, I'm the one who gets hurt. Brian and his girlfriend could care less.

Besides, I have already outdone myself in outwitting Brian. On one occasion I told him my car wasn't working and asked him to drive me to the lab for a blood test the next day.

Trying to sound quite casual, Brian inquired, "Which lab?"

His face turned red when I said, "Oh, the one about a mile from here with the red tile roof." This was Noreen's place of work.

"Why are you changing labs?"

"Oh," I explained, "the technician at the other place is rough when she puts the needle in. You know I don't like to be hurt."

"How do you know this new place is any better?" Brian asked with trepidation in his voice.

I said: "I hear they're very good and they make it easy for patients. Everyone in this lab, including the secretary and receptionist, are said to be very kind."

"Let me check my schedule," Brian mumbled. "I'll let you know."

When Marsha reaches into the car to retrieve the fish and garlic oil container, I say, "I think we're making a mistake. They're not worth it. Besides, can you just see the headlines? 'CRUSADING TV REPORTER IDENTIFIED AS PERPETRATOR OF FISH AND GARLIC OIL ATTACK ON OTHER WOMAN'S CAR ENGINE . . . SEEN LIMPING AWAY FROM THE SCENE WITH A WALKER.'"

This cracks Marsha up. "Are you sure?" she asks.

"Yes. Why bother? What goes around comes around."

We talk more seriously about divorce at lunch and, in particular, about my relationship with Brian's daughters. They should not be repositories of my anger toward their father. When Brian moved out, I wrote both of them letters:

When people grow apart, it's time for them to move on. That's what your father and I must now do.

But I want you to know that you are the most important people in his life and that he loves you very much. So do I and I will always be here if you need me.

They wrote back to tell me they loved me and could they still be *my girls.*

I'm lucky I had the checkbook in this relationship and that my career is solid. I tell Marsha, "It must be awful for women with small children, who have never worked and have no other means of support. I'm also lucky because I have a terrific family."

"They are really great," she agrees. "You all really stick together."

"Large families are tribal," I say. "I can always count on mine."

After listening to Brian's first conversation with Noreen, I called my mother and Karen to tell them I was going to get a divorce. Initially I did not let my other siblings know because, unlike Karen, who is the voice of reason, they would be wildly angry at Brian's betrayal. This would only fuel my rage.

Karen, concerned that I might strike out foolishly, came to Orlando to listen, console, and advise, helping me to think rationally, rather than emotionally, about the situation. Johnny arrived the following weekend to keep me calm and to exercise with me and, as always, to make me laugh.

By the time I reach home the giddy hysteria that earlier in the day was the buffer against the pain of a lost relationship is wearing off. I walk into the house, now devoid of Brian's presence, and the sadness deepens into melancholy.

Divorce is like a death. I am alone again. And I know it's over in other ways. Brian was not just my husband, but he is likely to be the last man who will ever know me intimately.

However, work never fails me and, better yet, my pal R.C. is back. I think of him as my personal angel. A few months after we stopped working together, R.C. suddenly appeared in my office one morning. He looked terrible and trembled as he sat down, saying, "I'm losing it. I need help."

I immediately called my former psychiatrist and arranged for him to meet R.C. at a drug treatment facility. R.C. was admitted that day and remained there for a month. Next, I got in touch with Mike Schweitzer to explain R.C.'s problem, that he was getting help but was worried he would lose his job. "Tell him not to worry," said Mike. "His job will be there."

During R.C.'s stay at the drug facility he called me several times to talk and to update me on his progress. He returned to work a changed person and told me he was saved and had become a born-again Christian. He was still clean a year later, and when I was looking for someone to replace Kenny, who had been promoted to a desk job, R.C. volunteered to come back.

I later learned that he did so because, when he saw my deteriorating condition, he thought it was his turn to help me. His work is, once again, first-rate. And he always tells me, "Don't worry, I'll take care of you, babe." He always does.

We are working on a story I call an exercise in consumer revenge. At least one hundred consumers, including me, received the same solicitation, leading us to believe we'd won a new Ford Mustang. To claim the car we had to take a tour and listen to a sales pitch about a time-share campground resort.

I rent a bus to take fifty-two people to the campground. Upon arrival we all go into the office. I announce to the campground manager: "I'm here with fifty-two people to pick up the Ford Mustangs we've won."

We don't get our cars, but as a result of my TV report, the Florida Secretary of State and the Attorney General's office mete out heavy fines for deceptive and misleading trade practices.

This story had such great impact that even today people stop to ask me if I ever got my car. And it made me realize that, while Brian gave me a path, I've achieved because of my talent and my hard work. My successes belong to me.

And the story is memorable for a more poignant personal reason: it is the last time I report a story standing on my feet.

———

MS is a disease of surprises. It is so cruel, like an abusive husband who beats up his wife and says, "I'm sorry, honey. I really didn't mean it. I'll be really good." And he is really good for a while and then, whop! he slams her again.

This is what MS does. It teases you, sometimes you feel pretty good, and then, when you least expect it, it knocks you out. This is a disease that sits back and says, "Ha, ha, ha, got you again." All the songs the TV station uses to promote me—"Catch me if you can" . . . "Every step you take, I'll be watching you . . ."—well, that's what I feel the MS is doing.

MS does not leave you alone and if you don't pay attention to it for a moment, it will get your attention. It's smarter than I; more vicious and more vindictive.

It doesn't care that it inconveniences me and it doesn't care that it prevents me from doing some of the work I would like to do, from doing some of the pleasurable things I would like to do.

It does not care that it robs me of sexuality or causes painful sensations in my legs; that it puts my back into spasms; and that I have to freeze all the time because if I get overheated my body won't function. This means that, in order to walk even a few steps, I must bring the air temperature down so low that I shiver and contract.

By June 1990, I can no longer stand up without a walker, and I suffer minor concussions from my frequent falls. When my mother visits and sees me hunched over a walker as I drag my feet behind me, she says, "I can't bear to watch you struggle so. Why won't you consider using a wheelchair periodically?"

"I'll crawl," I vow, "before I'll sit down."

I try to explain that a wheelchair means much more than a loss of mobility. It promotes bladder and bowel dysfunction; loose shoulder, hip, and knee joints; muscle spasms; and poor circulation. Above all, a wheelchair would take away my dignity, self-esteem, and independence, and I don't want to be eye level with other people's navels.

This conversation turns out to be prophetic. On June 15, 1990, I am in New York to see Labe Scheinberg. After his examination, he says, "Ellen, you're in a desperate situation. The MS is progressing. Your decline is so severe and rapid that you'll be in a wheelchair within a few months. Cytoxan chemotherapy for seven days, along with intramuscular shots of the steroid ACTH, is the only available treatment. If it works, it will slow down the progression."

Cytoxan, an immunosuppressive drug, is effective because MS is an autoimmune disease: the immune system is so strong it attacks itself; sort of the biological equivalent of friendly fire. This is the opposite of AIDS, where the immune system is too weak to fight off infections.

My previous 0 rating on the disability scale has climbed to 6.5. I now have severe chronic progressive multiple sclerosis. Until now I never believed the MS would get this bad. I am not so sure that this time I can come back. There is no choice—I have to try chemotherapy.

My condition reminds me of my father's rapid decline in the last week of his life. There we all stood, my sisters and brothers, my mother, and I, in the corridor outside his room, with his doctor. "How did it happen so fast?" we asked him.

"It's like water dripping off a table," his doctor explained. "It starts with one drop and, then, all of a sudden, more water is falling and there's a flood. It happens that fast."

I return to Orlando to organize my papers and arrange for Vicky to manage the house and look after Churchill and Beijing in my absence. And there are other loose ends I need to take care of before subjecting myself to something as drastic as chemotherapy. I want to resolve my feelings about Brian and the divorce.

I call Brian and tell him about the chemotherapy and he comes to my house to talk.

105

"Brian," I begin, "it was so unlike you to behave so badly. I don't understand why you continued to lie, knowing how important telling the truth is to me."

Glumly, Brian says, "I don't know. Part of it's the MS. And I met someone. I was wrong and I'm really sorry about it."

His eyes start to tear and he asks, "Do you blame me for the deterioration?"

"I think you bear great responsibility for it," I answer. "But it's done. And I want you to know that I don't hate you. I'm not even angry with you anymore. While I can't forgive your behavior, I forgive you."

On his way out the door, Brian hugs me and says, "Ellen, I'll always love you and I'll do anything to help."

With everything said, I am able to say good-bye to my marriage.

———

I stay with my mother at our family house for a few days before checking into the hospital. Ever practical and efficient, and remarkably energetic and still a working judge at seventy-four, she has already arranged for me to have around-the-clock nurses and any other amenities that will make me more comfortable. She also sets up a schedule for visits by my sisters and brothers so someone in the family will be with me at all times.

Having watched my father, her husband, go through chemotherapy, she finds my situation unbearable. Understanding her agony, I tell my mother it's not necessary for her to visit me at the hospital. I'll talk with her every day by phone.

To ward off the nausea from chemotherapy, I plan to smoke marijuana in the hospital. Although it is illegal, the evidence shows it is an effective antidote for nausea. Its usefulness has also been shown with glaucoma, relieving symptoms; with AIDS, increasing the appetite; and with MS, reducing muscle spasms and cooling down the body. For me it's particularly helpful because I am so heat-sensitive.

Clearly, I do not use marijuana to amuse myself; I don't smoke pot and giggle or watch movies with dazzling special effects. It is, indeed, a serious issue with me and I strongly believe that there are compellingly sound and humane reasons to legalize marijuana for medical purposes.

All the neurologists I've seen agree it has a salutary effect on MS patients and they would like to be able to write prescriptions for it. I don't talk too much about this because I want to protect people who buy it for me illegally. Meanwhile, I am hoping for a more reasonable government policy regarding this issue.

Jessica comes out to see me the night before I am due in the hospital. I'm so nervous that I drink two glasses of wine. When this doesn't relieve my anxiety, I smoke some pot. Certainly this doesn't help my balance, which is already bad from MS. My feet are so numb that when I stand up I forget to look where they are placed and I trip over my walker and fall.

I begin to laugh so hard that my body becomes a dead weight. So when Jessica tries to help me up, she ends up on the floor with me. Now, both of us are rolling around and laughing.

Hearing the commotion, my mother rushes into my room and, in a frantic voice, scolds, "Oh my God, you could have hit your head on the table, Ellen. The two of you are behaving like infants."

We are, but it makes us both feel better. My mother then says, "You're so thin, Ellen. How much do you weigh?"

"With or without the diapers?" I ask. "Actually, I'm giving Jessica a diaper so we can try out for the roles of Tweedledee and Tweedledum."

My mother, stifling a laugh, comments, "I assume the two of you find this very funny. But I think you should get off the floor and go to bed."

"Okay," I say, and then, putting on one of the gloves I use to keep my hand warm, I add, "Look, Michael Jackson in diapers." In bed that night, I have a dream:

> I am in a wheelchair going into a dusty tunnel when another
> chair bumps into me. I see a horrible-looking woman sitting in
> it. She has a lime-green face, like Kermit the Frog; big rubbery

red lips; giant yellow teeth; and wears a blond wig parted down the middle. She gives me this very shy grin, as if to say, "We're going in together, baby." On her lap is a thin black cane with a brass tip.

I try to maneuver away from her—not out of fright but because she is so hideous. I manage to get over to one side near a ledge and just as our chairs approach the tunnel, I jump out. She looks at me with desperation, drops her cane, and is propelled into the tunnel alone.

I pick up her cane and give it to the attendant in charge of the wheelchair ride: "Please give this to her when she comes out—she'll need it."

"No, you give it to her," he says.

I walk away: "I don't want it!"

I think the dream is a sign that, once again, I have defeated the MS. I have tricked it again.

————

On July 1, 1990, I am in a room on the neurology floor at Albert Einstein Hospital in the Bronx, preparing to start chemotherapy. Every time a doctor or a nurse comes in I put on a brave front, but, in fact, I am terrified. It is down to the bottom line—this disease has me. There is no healthy denial this time. I am now forced to actualize my MS; to stop thinking about myself in the third person.

Chemotherapy feels as if you put a piece of ice on your finger and then run it through your body. And, oh, the weakness it causes: I'm forty-five and I feel eighty. Every morning, my body is hydrated for several hours with fluid that is fed intravenously. This is followed by four hours of Cytoxan chemotherapy.

During the procedure, I drink six to eight quarts of water to flush out my system. My body is a faucet; the liquid goes out as quickly as it comes in. The flow is so constant that if my mother had not arranged for private nurses around-the-clock, a catheter would have been necessary. They change my diaper every thirty minutes—I am keeping Depend and Attends in business.

They give me a prescription for Marinol, marijuana in pill form, to control nausea, but it's too strong. So, instead, I smoke marijuana cigarettes in the bathroom every day before chemotherapy begins.

My family helps me get through this dreadful experience. Each of my siblings plays a different role.

As painful as my illness is for Patricia, my twin, she also believes it is unacceptable to capitulate to this feeling. But this kind of situation allows her to speak to the best part of herself: her kindness and gentleness, not always apparent to others.

In some way she also feels guilty that maybe, as the bigger, stronger twin, she got all the good genes. But I never think, *Why me instead of you?* Why would I wish this agony on anyone else—least of all my twin?

In my room Patricia asks me, "Why is this happening to you? Why not me?"

"Because," I joke, "I'm the one who put the thumbtack on Mrs. McEvoy's chair in the second grade."

My younger sister, Jessica, is the deliverer of joie de vivre, decorating my hospital room with enormous sunflowers, plants, and dolls. What a shame that we weren't close as little girls!

She brings the same wonderful eye that informs her photography to her wardrobe. And I am rapidly thinning it out because every time she walks into the room, she loses an outfit.

"I really like that blouse," I mention.

"It's yours," she says.

After a few days of my praising her outfits, Jessica puts her hands over her face and, in mock distress, pleads, "Oh, please don't say you like this dress. I'll end up naked at this rate."

Karen, the oldest, reads to me—magazine articles and short stories by William Trevor. As she rubs my head gently and pats my hand, it is as if she were telling me bedtime stories. My brothers, John and Judd, drift in and out of the room, bringing me flowers and jokes.

The kindness of my family soothes. I learn, just as I did on that July day a year ago, when I lay on the broiling hot cement for four hours, it is really all about love.

During my fourth evening in the hospital, while a lab technician tries to find a vein for a new intravenous needle, he keeps sticking me and I scream at him to stop. A woman enters my room: Dr. Angela Hegarty, a psychiatrist and neurology resident. She is just wonderful, just really nice, and she sits on the side of the bed, warms up my hand with hers, and puts it in warm water to get the veins to come up. I don't even whimper during the first two or three excruciating, bloody attempts because she is trying with such gentle intent.

I feel so comfortable with Angela that I tell her about my dream and how I avoided going through the tunnel with that awful-looking woman. I ask her what this means.

"You were confronting your own fear," she interprets. "You must go through the tunnel again."

We're interrupted by Labe, who comes to examine me. I guess the worst news is that I have the worst form of the disease; the best news is that I've got the best form of the worst form of the disease. Labe determines that I'm not weak because of bad balance. Rather, I have a problem with balance because I'm weak.

Labe tells me that suicide is the second leading cause of death in MS and he is very concerned that I am dangerously depressed. "Suicide will never be an option," I assure Labe, and tell him about my failed suicide and the white light.

Angela is still in the room and Labe asks if I want her to stay and talk. I do. Labe says good-bye and tells me he'll see me next week in his office.

Angela sits down on the bed again and we resume our discussion about my dream. She wants to know about my past and I tell her I grew up thinking I was ugly, fat, and stupid.

She says, "That person who went into the tunnel was the ugly, fat, and stupid part of you and that's why you think you deserve the MS." Next, she asks, "Who was the attendant at the tunnel?"

"I don't know."

"Well, that was your father, the one who taught you that you were ugly, fat, and stupid. The woman's face was green because she doesn't know how to use makeup. You have to go in and teach her." Angela instructs me to create and visualize a scenario. "Begin your journey when you're awake, before you go into the tunnel."

I say I will try to do this. I will do it.

I begin the visualization at three o'clock in the morning:

> Standing at the entrance of the tunnel, I can see the woman huddled in her chair. "Don't be frightened. Please wait there, I'm coming through to be with you." Then I turn to the attendant. "Daddy, let go. It's over. I'm no longer ugly, fat, and stupid. Clean the cane so I can bring it to the woman."
>
> When it's ready, I send the cane through the tunnel. "Please put it in front of you," I instruct her. "There's an abyss and I don't want you to go over it alone." Next, I send a shaft of light into the tunnel so I can find her and a golden, cleansing cloak for her to wear. I put on a purple, healing cloak, sit down in a chair, and ride into the tunnel. When I reach her, I tell her she is beautiful and, with a corner of her golden cloak, begin to clean her face.
>
> The woman who eventually emerges has clear white skin, beautiful teeth, and short, dark hair. She just looks so pretty and I put my arms around her and say, "Okay, it's time to go over the abyss. I don't know where we're going, but let's just jump." We land in the middle of a stream of warm water and I tell her what Angela counseled me: "You won't grow if you stay on one side of a stream, you have to swim down in the middle."
>
> I wash her with the warm water and send an iridescent, white light through her scalp and spinal cord to eradicate MS crud. I burn the residual waste to prevent MS from polluting anyone else. Then I wrap my arms around her; we spin around and become a yellow and purple cocoon. It breaks open when we reach a waterfall at the end of the river, transforming us into butterflies.

We float back down to the beginning of the tunnel and I tell her, "We have to go through the tunnel again. I don't know where it will take us. It could put us in a wheelchair, but we have to ride through to the end."

There, we find steps and I can see a patch of blue at the bottom: "This is it. I'm going to count down from ten." Our journey ends on a clear white beach with a bright blue sky, and unfettered by disease, we dance joyfully down the beach.

I open my eyes. It is five o'clock in the morning. I am out of denial. I'm not going to lie to myself anymore. MS won't take me down without a fight, but if I have to go into a wheelchair, I can handle it.

This experience changes me so profoundly that I feel complete and at peace. And my transformation is apparently noticeable to others. The staff nurses come into my room several times a day to talk with me. They also say they see a glow around me. No one notices when I leave the hospital by walker instead of by wheelchair.

Over the next two weeks the nurses who look after me at our family home see the walker and still say, "Who's the patient?" Nobody sees my disability.

A week after chemotherapy, I feel strong enough to go to a bookstore near our home. There I pick out five books including Lillian Hellman's *Scoundrel Time* because I want to reread a passage that is particularly appropriate at this time:

> I have written here that I have recovered. I mean it only in a worldly sense because I do not believe in recovery. The past, with its pleasures, its rewards, its foolishness, its punishments, is there for each of us forever, and it should be.
>
> As I finish writing about this unpleasant part of my life, I tell myself that was then, and there is now, and the years between then and now, and the then and now are one.

Chemotherapy has so weakened my bladder that I have little or no control when I have to urinate. The urge takes over just when I get to the counter to pay for my purchases.

Trying to avoid an accident, I ask the manager to direct me to the bathroom. "We don't have a bathroom," she says.

"Where do your employees go?"

"Well, it's a rule," she states matter-of-factly, "that customers cannot use the store's bathroom."

"But this is an emergency," I plead with her. "I just had chemotherapy. Can't you make an exception?"

"Sorry, that's the owner's rule."

At this point I think about leaving a puddle on the floor of the store. Instead, I leave all five books on the counter and stumble out to the car. I don't make it and wet my diaper.

It was such a terribly cruel thing for this woman to do and it humiliated me.

When I see Labe, he tells me it will be six months before he knows if the chemotherapy was successful. And he advises me, if I plan to return to Orlando, to do so within two weeks. After that my white blood count will drop so low that I'll be highly susceptible to infection.

He hugs me on the way out. "Oh, and by the way, Ellen, wash your hair so it's clean when it falls out."

My youngest brother, Judd, flies back with me to Orlando. He helps me choose a scooter and trade my Volkswagen Cabriolet convertible for a van with a lift.

———

It's Sunday morning . . . about 2 A.M., July 15. What is it, fifteen days since I went into the hospital for chemotherapy? This is a bitch! I'm tired of shielding people from the terrible agony of this disease. As I said, it's two o'clock in the morning. It just took me approximately half an hour to open a bottle of wine, get some cheese and crackers, and smoke a joint to stop the nausea that still lingers from chemotherapy.

What started as a minor inconvenience is now a major hassle. It is an appendage now: my name is Ellen Burstein MacFarlane, MS.

It's as if you can be left with just good moments—each one a small victory. When I walk down the hall, it's a sign the motor pathway is still active. When I collapse, it's a sign the pathway is closed. When I recover my strength, I think, *Okay, I'm okay, I haven't lost the use of my legs—it's still here. But one day it will be gone.*

My primary problem with mobility aids is that they are inconvenient. I could be walking down the hall reading a book instead of keeping my hands locked on a walker and my eyes on the path in front of me. And this is no great protection anyway because if I'm in a rush to get to the bathroom or if I turn around too quickly, I fall.

You win little battles and each individual has to make a choice about his or her own quality of life. What is worth the fight? I mean, I had acquired so many walkers and canes trying to accommodate the MS that I was all ready to start my own supply store. I behaved like my little dog Beijing: if I walk by and don't look at you, you won't notice I'm there. I thought if I got all these little aids, just everything possible, no one would notice my MS—they'd just kind of ignore it and then it would make it easier for me to ignore. So I hopped from one walker and cane to another.

Walking into a building, I immediately look for the location of the toilet. When I get dressed, I must account for an extra size because my diaper needs room. The accommodation is so enormous, I can't ignore it. It keeps saying, "Don't forget, I'm over here . . . I'm over here." You never know when you'll get hit. It's like Simon Says. "Do this," Simon says, "do that."

I just want the progression to stop. I want to look well right now. Please just give me a break for a little bit. I need a rest. I'll deal with it, I accept it, but just give me a little bit of a rest right now.

I've been wrong to shield people from the horror of this disease, and I apologize to those I ignored who were going through the terror of this, who thought I didn't understand. I didn't. No one can understand it until you go through it yourself.

So how do I begin again? First, I tell the truth . . .

Six weeks later when I comb my hair, it falls out in clumps. Within fifteen minutes I am bald. My mother is visiting.

Just as she did with the chemotherapy, my mother has, once again, organized a family brigade to visit me in Orlando; each one of my brothers and sisters arrive every other weekend.

She smiles when she sees my new look. "You look beautiful," she says. "I never realized you have such a pretty face."

"Even better, Mother," I say, "I can wash and dry my head in five seconds."

I am not ashamed of being bald and I decide not to wear a wig when I return to work: one, because it may make it easier for others who lose their hair from chemotherapy and I've already made enough accommodations to the MS. And, second and most important, it is consistent with my character to tell the truth, and the truth is I have no hair.

The station, however, insists I wear a wig. We compromise on a hat and a scarf. They air a two-part series on me to let the audience know how I spent my summer vacation, and they hire a producer to do field work for me.

In November I am the cover story of the *Orlando Sentinel*'s *Florida* magazine. There is a picture of R.C. standing behind me with his camera above my hairless head. The headline: "ELLEN MACFARLANE COMING AT YOU. . . . Nothing stops this consumer reporter in her quest to ambush creeps and swindlers—not threats, not slammed doors, not even multiple sclerosis." The writer, Mike Thomas, did a terrific job.

Within days of its publication, I receive, on average, thirty letters a day. People with MS share their experiences. Others send me information about cures, from vitamins to faith healing. They all say they're praying for me. I am delighted by a large manila envelope filled with letters from Mrs. Johnson's fourth-grade students at the Challenger Elementary School in Cocoa, Florida. A sample:

Dear Ellen:

I herd [*sic*] you were sick. I want you to get well. I think you're great on Channel 6 News. You are a nice woman.

I hope you get well soon. I am ten years old.

Your best friend,

Angela

There are also wonderful drawings of me, in every possible size, shape, and nationality. In one I am in a bikini on the beach in Hawaii holding a microphone. I answer each and every one of their letters, signing off, "Your best friend, Ellen."

Much to my surprise, I hear from a man who was convicted of grand theft after I exposed his activities as an unlicensed contractor:

Dear Ms. Ellen MacFarlane:

I don't write to talk about my case. I write to say thank you.

I was wrong in what I did. Please forgive me. I love and I respect you for what you did for me.

May the love of God always be with you forever. Take care of yourself.

I am enormously moved by his letter.

Equally surprising is a letter I receive from the previous general manager of the station (WFTV) that fired me because of a contract dispute back in 1985:

. . . And if I hadn't left WFTV, I daresay you'd still be there, doing your inimitable thing.

Keep on giving 'em hell, and may you be fully back on your feet soon!

I also hear from my friend Kathy Stilwell, who is now bedridden. We talk by phone at least once a week. But I can no longer bear to see her because now, when I look at her, I am looking at my future.

At this year's Ellen MacFarlane Walk for MS, unknown to me, I capture the attention of a man who is newly diagnosed with MS. He gets me on the phone at the station by using the name of a mutual friend and tells me he loves the symphony and plays the violin, as I once did. Because he sounds so distraught about the MS on the phone I agree to meet and talk with him. Patricia, who is staying with me, knows that I am trying to make it easier for people who have MS and suggests I invite this man to my house for lunch.

What a mistake! He brings me a ten-page, single-spaced autobiography, several books, a tape of a recent violin recital that he dedicated to me, and three soppy cards expressing his love for me.

Patricia and I are getting nervous and she says, "He's so obsessed with you if you said, 'Please pass the salt,' he would find this quite fascinating."

After he leaves me a phone message saying that it's been "three hours, two minutes, and thirty seconds since he's talked to me," I must insist that he not call me again. I receive a few more letters before he gives up.

Before the year is out, I make my first public appearance in my scooter (motorized wheelchair) at a supermarket.

Jessica, who is visiting me, comes along, and she challenges me to a race. Standing up in my scooter, I zoom in and out of the aisles and, so carried away, I crash into the meat counter and fall over.

When people rush over to help me, they find me laughing on the floor. Quoting Labe, I tell them, "It's the 'NK' factor—I'm a natural klutz."

Slightly embarrassed, I get up and reduce my traveling speed. MS may slow me down, but it doesn't change who I am.

I'm still in the race.

CHAPTER 10

How Do I Stay on My Feet?

1991

I refuse to sit down. In January 1991 I hear about a new medicine, 4-Aminopyridine (4-AP), that may be helpful in improving functions for MS patients. For the moment, while awaiting FDA approval, it is available only in liquid form from Bulgaria.

Dr. Herman Weinreb, a neurologist at New York University Medical Center, is conducting a research project on patients with the 4-AP. In the lobby of his building, wheelchairs are available but I choose instead to use my walker.

This is possible only because I am wearing my AFO braces in my sneakers. Made out of plastic, they fit around the back of my lower legs and under my feet and keep the front half of my foot at a ninety-degree angle. This prevents me from tripping over my feet when I walk, a common MS mobility problem called "drop foot."

Dr. Weinreb is a pudgy man, with rosy cheeks, in his early forties.

His manner is both earnest and caring. And when I ask him why MS is his specialty he says, "Because it's such a mysterious disease." After an extensive examination, he discusses the ongoing trials on new drugs for MS. None of them seems to work on my form, severe chronic progressive. I ask him about 4-AP.

He tells me it is not a cure, but in some cases it increases energy and improves function. The 4-AP is a potassium channel blocker: sodium goes into each cell in the body and potassium comes out. When the myelin (coating) is destroyed all the potassium leaks out. By blocking the outflow of potassium the 4-AP facilitates nerve conduction among the damaged cells. Weinreb tells me it works best for MS patients who are heat-sensitive, which I am, and those who have eye problems. There are no known side effects unless the maximum dosage, four vials a day, is exceeded. Then seizures might result.

"I don't know if the 4-AP will help you," Weinreb says, "but it's worth a try." The medicine is contained in a primitive glass vial. To open it, he files off the tip of the vial and pours its contents into orange juice, the recommended way to take it, and hands the paper cup to me.

Swallowing the potion, I imagine, just as I did as a child believing I could fly, I will be running down the hallway in a few minutes. I am convinced the 4-AP is a panacea for a jogger sidelined by MS.

Nothing happens. My sisters, who are along, are speechless and I do not know what to tell them or myself. I am horribly disappointed. So much for being out of denial and setting unrealistic expectations.

Dr. Weinreb gives me a supply of the 4-AP, requests I take blood tests quarterly to check my liver, and that I make periodic visits so he can monitor my condition on the medication.

Back home I am becoming a designer for the disabled, modifying and customizing my walkers and other aids into fashionable objects. My younger sister, Jessica, meanwhile, visits and gives me snazzy, tricolored phosphorescent shoelaces with matching sequin sneakers that amuse me and lift my spirits. I also wear bright-colored leg warmers that match my outfits, over the braces. I think that by camouflaging my walking aids it won't look as if I need them.

A few weeks later, when I call Weinreb to say the 4-AP isn't working, he tells me to increase the dosage to the maximum four vials a day. The effect is immediate. Within a minute I have increased strength and coordination.

After Patricia sees Weinreb to replenish my 4-AP supply she tells me about her conversation with him. His answer to why he became a physician: "I don't like to see anyone suffer." When she inquired if anyone in his family had MS or a related illness, he gave a very moving answer. "Not that . . . but my parents were in the Holocaust." For the worst MS cases, he explained in relation to the 4-AP, "it can mean the difference between being a complete shut-in and having some contact with other people. It may give him or her just enough energy to dial someone's telephone number to speak to one person the entire day."

Then, Weinreb, physician and son of Holocaust survivors, remarked, softly, "It's the little things that count."

He is right. And he is the first person I've met who doesn't have MS and yet really understands the critical importance of little victories.

My Type A personality is now trapped in a Type B body. At work, inside the station, I am still able to get around on foot with the support of a walker and a quad cane (it has a wide base), and by wall walking, but in the field, I need to travel by three-wheeled motorized scooter. In February 1991, Susan Reed, a writer for *People* magazine, calls to say she read the *Florida* magazine cover story about me and would like to do an "On the Job" feature story.

People reporter Meg Grant and photographer Acey Harper come to Orlando and go with me to the county courthouse, where I, in my scooter, zoom down the corridors in pursuit of a cheat named John Lewis Nuccitelli.

This man is an expert at "equity skimming": he scouts out homeowners facing foreclosure; he lies to them about assuming their mortgages in exchange for a signed quit-claim deed and then rents the properties he doesn't own. He takes one-thousand-dollar cash deposits up front from his unsuspecting tenants, who are later evicted when the banks foreclose.

Hiding his face with a newspaper, Nuccitelli does a fast trot to the courtroom for his arraignment on organized fraud and grand theft charges. But he can't outrace me and my microphone. I put my scooter in high gear.

R.C. gets it all on tape. "John, these are very serious charges," I state as I rev up my scooter to five miles an hour. "Why do you collect rent on homes you don't own? Why do you lie to your tenants? Do you have anything to say?"

He refuses to answer but I'll be back with my scooter for his trial. I love the sound of the engine cranking up.

A bystander in the courthouse is quoted in the *People* story, which appears in late April: "She [Ellen] sure stays on their butts." The article is well written and very flattering and it amuses me to imagine that everyone who was ever mean to me in grade school might read it.

The *People* feature results in an appearance for me on the CBS-TV Morning News. Co-anchor Paula Zahn does a highly sensitive and intelligent interview about the emotional pain of living with MS and how important it is to remain both productive and hopeful.

In a strange way, the publicity about my achievements, in spite of MS, gives me the approval I sought as a child. It is also gratifying to receive national confirmation, beyond my local celebrity in Orlando, of how good I am at what I do.

However, I still have multiple sclerosis. And I'm still struggling to stay on my feet, out of a wheelchair.

A friend sends me a copy of the March 18, 1991, *New York* magazine. The cover story, by Tony Schwartz, is about cardiovascular surgeon Dr. Irving I. Dardik. The headline: "MAKING WAVES . . . CAN DR. IRV DARDIK'S RADICAL EXERCISE THERAPY REALLY WORK MIRACLES?"

Basically, this doctor claims his stress/recovery regimen, labeled Superesonant Wavenergy (SRWE), will correct imbalances in the immune system that cause such chronic illnesses as MS. Pendulum swings that are created by quickly raising and lowering the heart rate through exercise cycles eventually restore the body's equilibrium and banish MS as well as other chronic and fatal illnesses.

The story is, in fact, a tome—an article of uncommon length, nine pages and incredibly adulatory. Dardik's credentials seem impeccable: a highly respected cardiovascular surgeon with a private practice in Englewood, New Jersey; the inventor of an arterial graft; former chairman of the United States Olympic Committee's Sports Medicine Council. And the fact that he is profiled in a major mainstream magazine lends credence to his theory.

MS is a neurological, not a cardiovascular, problem but it is believed to be an autoimmune disease and Dardik's theory using the heart as a window to balance the immune system to cure chronic illness seems reasonable.

Dardik, a former track star, says his stress/recovery program is derived from working with athletes; he believes athletes stress their bodies too much and people with chronic illnesses don't stress their bodies enough.

According to the article, "Dardik has submitted a paper to several journals, but with no hard data and a radical thesis, he has yet to find a taker . . ." And "Dardik's unified theory isn't likely to win wide acceptance by the Scientific Establishment anytime soon." In addition, "What's harder to dismiss is his clinical success in treating patients with chronic illnesses . . ."

The article contains the subjective, anecdotal success stories of some six patients with ailments ranging from enteritis to MS. While he acknowledges that his patients experience setbacks, Dardik is also quoted telling one MS patient, "Things don't just get all better and stay that way, but you'll never fall back to where you were when you started."

In this case the forty-five-year-old woman had a recurrence of her MS symptoms: extreme fatigue, constant diarrhea, and the loss of significant function in her left leg, which had locked at the knee. But according to the *New York* piece, "sure enough, two weeks later [after the setback] the woman had another breakthrough and was able to walk an even longer distance, pain-free and without fatigue."

This woman, to be sure, does not have severe chronic progressive MS like me but, nevertheless, I am hooked by the statement "you'll never fall back to where you were when you started." Dardik, *New York* magazine also reports, may be his own best test case: through his SRWE program, he recovered completely from ankylosing spondylitis, a degenerative disease of the connective tissue of the spine, which had earlier crippled his father.

All of this background, with positive coverage in *New York* magazine, as opposed to, say, the *National Enquirer,* gives Dardik's SRWE a patina of respectability. And to me, with my deteriorating condition, "you'll never fall back to where you were when you started" sounds like a victory when it comes to MS.

At the very least, I want to learn more about Dardik's SRWE program and talk personally with him. To his credit, he appears to be the opposite of a "hard sell" businessman-doctor; his phone number is unlisted and it is only through a former high school friend, whose late father was also a physician, that I am able to reach him.

And, even then, there is no guarantee I'll get into the program. When I call his unlisted number, his secretary tells me that, as a result of the magazine article, there is a waiting list of two thousand chronically ill people and she does not know if Dardik can fit me in.

I send a letter:

May 6, 1991

Dear Dr. Dardik,

I felt very encouraged after reading the *New York* magazine article about your Superesonant Wavenergy theory and your success with those who refuse to give in to multiple sclerosis.

I have the most severe form of chronic progressive MS and have been able to stay on my feet with the help of a physical therapist and an intensive program of daily exercise. I have always thought that people sit down too easily when their mobility is impaired and I believe that exercise is the most viable treatment.

Enclosed are two articles about my efforts to treat MS as an inconvenience. While I won't go down without a fight, I'm presently having difficulty maintaining "muscle memory."

I will call you next week to see if it's possible for me to set up an appointment with you for a consultation. I would be very grateful for any time and consideration you can give me.

Sincerely,

Ellen Burstein MacFarlane

Dardik, who is in his office the next time I call, tells me that he's been really busy and he hasn't been able to read my letter.

I flatter him. "I just know you are right."

"I *know* I am right," he answers, "but it takes a year to get rid of MS, you will have to be up in New York for at least a few months, and it will cost a lot of money."

Nowhere in the magazine article is there any mention of money—save for the writer's praise about Dardik's giving up a highly lucrative surgery practice "to sit broke in a library" for several years researching his theory. My guess is that it will cost thirty to fifty thousand dollars.

Not only am I willing to pay any amount of money to get well, I am also prepared to give up my work, which is so crucial to me, for a year. I can afford to put my job on hold because I know I will be able-bodied again.

When I tell Dardik that time and money won't be a problem for me, he says, "I'll read your letter and get back to you."

The next evening he calls me. "This is Irv," he says. "I read the articles. You're something else."

He says he can definitely cure me but I have to wait a bit: "Look, I'll be set up in a month or two."

"I can't wait," I say.

"Okay," Irv answers simply.

We agree to meet in New York City in June. I am excited by his promise to cure me.

———

I can't take Churchill and Beijing to New York with me, I don't want to put them in a kennel for the next five months, and unfortunately, my housekeeper/aide Vicky Medina can't stay at my house with them.

Brian and I have joint custody of Churchill and Beijing and because he has been very helpful since the chemotherapy, I decide to ask him. It might help him as well; he lost his job a few months ago and had to sell the New Smyrna Beach condo.

I am relieved when Brian agrees to dog- and house-sit while I'm gone. During our phone conversation, I suddenly realize I have no residual rage, that I'm over him, and I am no longer upset about the divorce.

I tell him and his reaction is surprising.

"What do you mean?" he asks.

"Well, it means you're my friend—you're just my friend."

In the evening, Brian calls again. "This is your friend calling," he announces.

"Are you upset about what I said?" I ask.

"I think so."

"Why?"

"Because," Brian says, "I feel like you're still my wife."

In some way his words comfort me, but I am still relieved that he's no longer my husband.

June 10, 1991, is my last day at work. On the six o'clock news, I say good-bye to my viewers:

> I did not want to leave for the summer without talking to you professionally and personally. First, let me review some of the ways you can protect yourself from cheats.
>
> Please don't believe you won a car if you get an urgent award notice . . . And never give your credit card number to telephone solicitors.
>
> Check with your local building department about a contractor's license before you hire him.
>
> Don't buy a used car "as is" or at least have it checked out by a mechanic. Don't take a new car off a dealer's lot unless financing has been approved.

Don't sign a contract to build or buy a house without having it reviewed by a lawyer. Read the small print before you sign any contract and make sure you get a copy.

Although I won't be reporting this summer, my office will continue to take your calls and answer your letters.

Now . . . On a more personal note, I want you to know how much I appreciated your calls and letters about my health. Your kindness, concern, encouraging words, and prayers often overwhelmed me.

Your generous hearts helped me get through a painful and difficult time and I thank you with all my heart.

Please watch out for the bad guys. I'll be watching too and I'll let you know.

My colleagues surprise me with a farewell party in the studio. I cry as I tell them that I'll be walking when I return in the fall.

CHAPTER 11

You'll Be Walking Within a Year

Summer 1991

I am on a plane going to New York, where Dr. Irving I. Dardik is going to cure me of MS. Last year, at this time, I was flying up to New York to learn that a wheelchair was imminent and chemotherapy was my only option.

On Tuesday, June 11, the day before meeting Irv, I am examined by Scheinberg. My condition is worse; on the disability scale of 0 (minimal to no disability) to 10 (death), I am still 6.5 and closing in on a 7.

"Labe," I say, "please tell me the truth. What is ahead for me? I need to know the worst-case scenario."

"Within a few years, you'll be quadriplegic," Labe replies. "But don't worry, this won't happen. You know I'll do everything possible to cure you. Until then, we can always do another round of chemotherapy."

To me, this is such an inadequate answer, such a toxic solution. I won't put my body through it again.

"Okay, what's the best-case scenario?" I ask Labe.

"You'll be in a scooter or wheelchair for the rest of your life."

"I will defy that," I exclaim.

"You can defy it all you want," Labe says with a hint of frustration in his voice, "but it doesn't change your condition."

I am furious with Labe. He doesn't understand that I won't compromise. I refuse to settle for mobility in a scooter.

I ask if he read the *New York* magazine cover story on Dr. Dardik's Superesonant Wavenergy theory. He has.

"What do you think?" I ask.

Labe shrugs. "Whatever works."

In a way, I feel sorry for Labe. He has devoted his entire adult life to MS and when I walk into his office in six months, he'll think, *For what?* . . . He spent all these years and Irv finds the cure.

———

I am staying with my younger sister, Jessica, in her apartment in the East Sixties in New York City. This is preferable to our family home on Long Island, which is not accessible and where I would be treated as a disabled child rather than a forty-six-year-old adult. Also, in Manhattan, I will go out with Jessica and her friends and stop hiding from people.

To make it easier for both of us, Jessica arranges for the building superintendent's wife to cook, clean, and be available to me during the day. Mary Ann, who is from Malta, is a kind, thoughtful, and patient woman and I feel comfortable with her.

On June 12, 1991, I meet Dr. Irving I. Dardik for the first time. He arrives at Jessica's apartment at 11 A.M. with his chief therapist, Michele Weiss. Dressed in shorts and a T-shirt, Irv looks a decade younger than his fifty-five years.

For the next two hours, he explains his Superesonant Wavenergy program, SRWE; basically, this involves exercise/recovery cycles that are designed to reactivate a static immune system so it can eliminate MS. He also tells me about his ALS, MS, and cancer patients who will be free of disease within a year.

Irv is both charismatic and compelling. This is a man who has a passion about his work.

Irv assures me, "The myelin [coating] around the cells is not gone, just thinned out and, therefore, is recoverable."

Several times during his dissertation, Irv emphasizes that he's not talking about a remission, which means the MS can come back. Rather, he says, enthusiastically, this is a cure and I will be walking within a year. He also tells me the cycles will cause skin rashes and tingling sensations and while there will be occasional down times, they are expected and only temporary. And, when my body bounces back, I will be better than ever.

I will exercise five days a week and recover for two, when I'll have to stay indoors and rest. The cycles will be a combination of what Irv calls "easies," such as standing up a few times or raising my arms, and more strenuous exercises using a trampoline, rower, and stationary bicycle.

I will do as many as thirty exercise cycles in one day: thirty seconds to two minutes of intense exercise to quickly shoot my heart rate up to a specific number; then I'll stop suddenly and sit or lie down to quickly lower it.

While this is the core of Irv's program, he will also use other techniques to vary my heart rate:

24- and 48-hour fasts

sun/shade cycles; 2 minutes of sun/2 minutes of shade, repeated 5 times

hot/cold shower cycles; 90 seconds of extremely hot water/90 seconds of ice-cold water, three repetitions at least once a day . . .

Irv says once I can get my heart rate to jump from the 60s to the 160s and then back down to the 60s within a few minutes, I'll walk.

If anyone can sniff out liars, it is certainly me. But there is nothing suspicious about Dr. Irving I. Dardik. I just know he has the answers and that he can cure me.

At the very least, as he claims in the *New York* magazine cover story, the MS won't get worse. This is good enough for me with severe chronic progressive MS approaching a 7 rating on the disability scale.

I am excited when Irv says he has a real interest in my case and that he will make it a priority. "You are a real challenge, a test case," he tells me. Because my form of MS, severe chronic progressive, means a steady downhill course without remissions, my recovery, he explains, can be nothing short of a 100 percent cure.

For the first time since the MS put me into the scooter, my hope outweighs my despair.

Before leaving, Irv talks privately with me about money, confiding his plans to set up a foundation and that, even now, he takes cases for free. However, in my case, he says, the cost is one hundred thousand dollars for a year of treatment and lifetime follow-ups because I am the equivalent of three patients and need his full-time attention: "I will not be able to take on additional patients because I'm going to be hands-on, five days a week, working one-on-one with you." Irv tells me that fifty thousand dollars is to be paid up front, twenty-five thousand in September and twenty-five thousand in January. He wants me to discuss the financial arrangements with his second wife, Alison, as he prefers to focus entirely on the program.

I cannot afford the fee all on my own and will have to ask my mother for help. It's a lot of money, but I'm desperate.

Treatment will begin Monday, June 17, 1991, and Irv instructs me to get exercise equipment: a Schwinn Airdyne bike; the Concept II Rower; a trampoline. To expedite delivery he gives me phone numbers to call: "Tell them you're one of Dr. Dardik's patients."

His one-hundred-thousand-dollar fee does not include this equipment, which costs about fifteen hundred dollars. I will also have to purchase a Polar heart monitor/watch from Irv for three hundred and twenty dollars, as well as a second watch and laptop computer from other vendors for over two thousand dollars. This is necessary, Irv says, so my heart rate, which the watches will record twenty-four hours a day, at five-, fifteen-, or sixty-minute intervals, can be downloaded into the laptop and sent to Irv's computer for his analysis. This, he says, is how he'll determine which heart rate numbers I should reach the next day. He will also arrange for me to get weekly blood tests.

"You're gonna be sick of seeing us," Irv threatens with a chuckle in his voice.

I ask Jessica, who listened in only briefly, what she thinks of Irv and his program. She is noncommittal, careful not to dampen my enthusiasm. Always, she wants me to feel hope.

My mother and my other siblings balk at what seems like an exorbitant fee for an unproven treatment. I insist that Irv's theory is valid; that he has excellent medical credentials; and that there is no cure forthcoming from orthodox medicine. Besides, what are my options? Another round of chemotherapy, which didn't work the first time?

"Believe me," I tell my mother and siblings, "with the kind of investigative reporting I do, I'd be the first to know if Irv is pulling a scam. After all the liars and cheats I've exposed, I have built-in radar for this sort of thing. If I saw any reason to doubt Irv, I'd be the first one on his case."

Jessica is my witness, albeit reluctantly, repeating to everyone exactly what Irv said to her when she called about the hundred-thousand-dollar fee: "I can cure Ellen, and it costs this much because Ellen is the equivalent of three patients and needs my full-time attention. I will be hands-on, five days a week, working one-on-one with Ellen and will not be able to take on more patients."

Additionally, Jessica reports, Irv wants to be certain I am definitely staying at her apartment because he has other patients in the area and it will be easier to come back and forth during the day to do the exercise cycles with me.

When I tell my mother about Irv's fee schedule, fifty thousand dollars up front and two twenty-five-thousand-dollar payments within

six months, she says, "Quite honestly, I've never heard of such a financial arrangement on the part of any doctor. It makes no sense. I
want to discuss it with Cary [the family financial counselor]."

I am extremely worried that if my family protests, Irv will just decide not to work with me. I know it's a lot of money, hard-earned by
my late father and my mother, who is working as a court mediator
since her mandated retirement from the bench this year, but by now
I am completely sold on Irv's program. What other hope is there? As
Labe says, "a few years to quadriplegic."

I just know Irv has the answer. All the other chronically ill people
on the waiting list can't be wrong either. Only they and I really know
how Irv can help us. It is something so private, inside yourself, and by
doubting, you only hurt yourself. I believe his promise, "You'll be
walking within a year." And even if his cure is only a placebo effect,
what difference does it make? All that matters is that it works.

My mother, with her judicial expertise, is quite clearly mistrustful
of Irv's financial demands. But she will never say no to my hope, and
she reasons that, by my own sheer will and in spite of Irv, maybe I will
get well. She tells me she'll work it out.

Reassured, I immediately order all the exercise equipment.

I am uncomfortable about taking over Jessica's apartment. I know
I would hate it if somebody moved into my two-room apartment,
blocked my access to the bathroom, took over my bedroom and
turned it into a gym. But Jessica insists she wants to do this for me. I
really love her.

The following day, Thursday, June 13, 1991, Irv calls: "Let's not
wait until Monday. Why not get started as soon as possible. I'll see
you tomorrow, Friday, instead."

Irv arrives at 8 A.M. along with Michele and one of his patients, a
young woman named Jo, who says Irv cured her of bulimia. She looks
just wonderful and I am infused with even greater hope about Irv's
curing me.

For three hours, Irv and Michele lead me through some exercises
designed to bring my heart rate up and down: lift each leg twice . . .
recover; walk back and forth across Jessica's bedroom floor with my

walker . . . recover; rest for thirty minutes; stand up three times . . . recover.

My heart rate fluctuates between 77 and 103, which, according to Irv, is great news. His reason: if I had high numbers he couldn't help me.

Michele remarks that I'm more mobile than other MS patients because, she says, "You're relaxed about it."

Irv is ecstatic and exclaims, "I'm going to put the MS Society out of business! You know you'll be walking again!"

"How soon?" I ask.

Irv replies, "Probably by November."

"Will I be able to run?" I ask.

"Once you can walk, it follows that you'll be able to run."

Irv and Michele say good-bye and as they open the door to leave, Irv turns and with a smile spreading across his face, he tells me, "You know, Ellen, I'm going to cure you!"

"Irv, I have always believed that I would get everything back. Today, I know it."

I feel as if he has just told me, "Here, Ellen, I'm giving you back your life."

When Irv and Michele leave, I go with Jessica to her doctor. She is gone for an hour and while waiting, I fall asleep. I'm so exhausted that I collapse when we get back to the apartment. When Irv calls that evening and I tell him what transpired, he explains how that will happen and how I have to follow exactly what they tell me to do because too much exercise can cause an exacerbation.

We also talk briefly about "mind over body" and holistic medicine. Like Bernie Siegel, the surgeon/healer, I firmly believe that a positive attitude can speed up and even cure chronic and life-threatening illnesses. However, if it doesn't, what then? Is someone to feel even more dejected?

At a recent Bernie Siegel workshop and lecture in Orlando, I and the other participants drew pictures of ourselves. Then Siegel asked me, "How did you draw yourself? Were you sitting in a chair?"

"No," I said, "I was standing up."

I don't perceive myself as disabled so it never occurred to me to draw myself sitting down. Even in my dreams, I'm always on my feet.

I, personally, learned a great deal that day about moving through illness. And I felt really good about myself when people with life-threatening diseases hugged me, said they loved me and were praying for me. It was a wonderful affirmation of the impact I've had in the community.

But Irv's program is more tangible than a theory that suggests that by believing you'll get better, you will. With Irv's Supersonant Wavenergy program, I will be cured.

The next day, Saturday, at 8:30 A.M., Michele arrives alone to work with me. She says Irv will see me next week. Michele tells me about her background, which I find quite interesting. She studied ballet and ran track until she developed problems with her knees.

She was born with primary immune deficiency and takes a slew of drugs daily to ward off infections which are life-threatening. Michele tells me that she graduated from Oberlin College and then began doctoral studies in biochemistry at the Rockefeller Institute. But because of her illness and frequent hospitalizations, Michele says she had to drop out. Next, she worked in a cardiac care and rehabilitation center. She recently quit because she was so upset by the way they treated people.

Michele tells me that although Irv's SRWE program contradicts everything she learned in her own medical training, nonetheless she is hooked and is convinced of the validity of his wave theory. Michele also follows the program, believing it will keep her healthy and out of the hospital.

We do some exercises on the trampoline along with the rower and bike that arrived within forty-eight hours of my calling and using Dardik's name.

I also do deep knee bends, going up on my toes and down on my heels. My heart rate stays between 72 and 106, which Michele assures me is normal at the outset and with time the swings will be greater.

Sunday is a recovery day, so after Michele leaves, I go with Mary Ann, the housekeeper/aide, and Jessica to the family house on Long

Island. As Michele has instructed, I spend fifteen minutes outdoors: in the sun until I feel my body overheating, and then in shade to recover. My heart rate climbs to 111 in thirty seconds of sun, drops to 97 in the shade, and 78 when I go back inside the house.

When I tell my family about Michele's immune deficiency disorder, they think her story is bizarre. I disagree. To my thinking, the circumstance of Michele's living with a chronic illness can only make her more understanding of what I am going through.

Monday, while I nap, Jessica calls Irv's wife, Alison, to discuss the fee: "Alison, we would like Ellen to do the program and she wants to do it. Irv says the cost is one hundred thousand dollars."

"Yes," Alison answers, "that's correct."

Jessica continues, "We prefer to pay Irv twenty-five thousand dollars quarterly."

Alison's response: "It's one hundred thousand dollars up front. This is not negotiable."

Jessica is shocked: "But Irv said it would be fifty thousand dollars up front."

Again, Alison tells her: "It's one hundred thousand dollars up front. This is not negotiable."

Jessica then tries a new approach. "We're not poor, but we certainly don't have Rockefeller money or anything remotely close to that. And it's not that my mother or any of us don't believe Irv has the cure, but, as you know, someone with a chronic illness requires lifetime care. I am sure you can understand that if something goes wrong and Irv doesn't cure Ellen's MS, the one hundred thousand dollars would be meaningful to us in the long term."

Alison is unmovable: "It's not negotiable."

Jessica then asks, "Much as I wouldn't want this to happen, what if something happens to Irv, he becomes ill or dies? I'm sorry, but would there be a refund?"

Normally, Alison tells Jessica, they don't give refunds but she'll make an exception if that is a condition of getting the one hundred thousand dollars up front.

Jessica ends the conversation thus: "There will be a lot of resistance from our family financial adviser, and if I were you, I'd come to some reasonable agreement with me now."

I excuse the non-negotiable demand because I just think it is Alison and Irv's way of preventing buyer's remorse as well as ensuring a patient's commitment to getting well and staying with the program. And although I repeatedly warn consumers not to pay money up front, especially without a contract, somehow I don't think I'm vulnerable. I guess that I believe that being part of a family that includes judges and attorneys, along with my expertise as an investigative consumer journalist, gives me immunity against crooks.

I am greatly relieved when our family financial adviser manages to negotiate a schedule of $50,000 up front with monthly payments over the next five months of $8,333.33. The latter sum, calculated by Alison down to the cent, vaguely amuses my family.

On June 24, late in the afternoon, my mother is in the city to visit me at Jessica's apartment and to meet Irv. He arrives in shorts and a T-shirt, having just done exercise/recovery (stopping and starting) cycles on his run from Penn Station: a distance of seventy blocks and four crosstown streets.

Speaking privately with Irv, my mother issues a caveat: "All I ask is that you keep your promises to my daughter and do not disappoint her. She has complete faith in you and I'm willing to do anything to help her. Ellen has told me she has such confidence in you and that she expects to be jogging in November."

To which Irv, chuckling over my positive spirit and fierce ambition to get well, says: "Ellen won't be running by November but she'll be walking by March. And she'll never be worse than she is now."

I can tell that my mother is not impressed. Nor does she understand Irv's Supersonant Wavenergy theory and tells him so in so many words.

Within a week of receiving his first payment, fifty thousand dollars, Irv begins to reduce his direct contact with me both by phone and in person. However, he consistently assures me, when we do talk, that I will be cured and walking soon.

I am becoming accustomed, anyway, to Michele, who comes in his stead and whom I regard as a potential friend. She is a real cheer-leader, though, and I find her chirpy expressions, like "Oooh, way to go," sort of idiotic.

Within the month, one of Irv's MS patients, who was profiled in the article about Irv, turns up at Jessica's apartment to talk with me. She has no visible signs of MS, still further proof of Irv's cure. She claims that Irv's program eliminated her bladder problems and stopped her need to use marijuana for relieving spasticity and muscle spasms. The following week, at Irv's insistence, I stop smoking mar-ijuana and drinking any alcohol, including wine. I will not use either again for almost a year.

At the end of July, I get a call from a representative of "Real Peo-ple," the former hit TV series. The show is being revised and will fo-cus on people who make a difference. They read the *People* article and want to include a feature on me in the pilot. The producer sends Willard Scott to interview me and arranges for R.C. to fly to New York to be included in the story. During the taping, Irv comes to Jes-sica's apartment to do cycles with me and, later, in the interview, I en-dorse him as the doctor who can cure MS. Ultimately, the segment is dropped from the final lineup because attorneys for my station are still litigating a case involving a promotional spot they did about my work.

I continue to take Cylert to control MS fatigue, but by early Au-gust, after just two months of exercise cycles, I have so much energy that I am able to cut the dosage in half. I am gaining strength; my feet are no longer numb; I stop using a brace on my left foot; and for the first time since the MS diagnosis in 1986, I can feel the floor be-neath my bare feet.

Clearly, Irv's program works!

Also in August, Irv takes me, Michele, and Tony Schwartz, the writer of the *New York* magazine cover story, to Princeton to see a meditation and relaxation specialist. There, we put on headphones to listen to New Age music while reclining on a vibrating bed. Irv and

Michele encourage me to use my walker this day, which puts a severe strain on my neck, back, and right shoulder as I have to lean on it and over it all day in order to walk.

This, as well as doing arm exercises on the Schwinn Airdyne bike, causes irreparable damage: a herniated disc; lower back, neck, and shoulder pain; severe weakness and tendinitis in my right arm.

Except for occasional sun/shade cycles, which are also supposed to produce a pendulum effect with my heart rate, Irv does not permit me to go outside because hot weather will exacerbate my MS.

Even when I take a bad fall and hit my head on the hard tile floor in Jessica's bathroom, which causes a severe headache, Irv instructs me not to go outside the building to see a neurologist. His reasoning: it's too hot outside. Jessica then arranges for me to be examined by a doctor who has an office in her building, but when I call Irv to tell him he refuses to rescind the order.

He assures me that I do not have a concussion, only a migraine that will go away, and within the year, the MS will be gone as well.

My mother visits and I ask Jessica not to mention my fall. She obliges. MS forces me to stand my ground. The more power I lose in my body, the more important it becomes for me to keep control of my beliefs and decisions.

Remarkably, in view of our family history of meddling in each other's lives, all my sisters and brothers are showing uncommon self-restraint by not expressing their thinly veiled skepticism about Irv.

Whenever I remark on the benefits of Irv's therapy, as I frequently do, all they say is, "We're glad. Good. All that matters is that you believe in him."

I do. My migraine disappears by morning. Better yet, I am starting to feel as if the MS may be retreating too.

In early September, Mary Ann has an appendectomy and won't be able to return to work for at least six weeks. I am beginning to feel I need some country air. Also, I feel Jessica is mistrustful of Irv and I want to avoid any questions about him. So, with Irv's approval and encouragement, I move to our family home on Long Island. Jessica gets me settled at the house. I'll still see her quite a lot, but I am going to miss her and our nightly conversations—and the flowers, chocolates, or stuffed animals she brings me almost daily.

There, the pain in my right arm and neck becomes so severe that I have to consult an orthopedist, who injects cortisone, prescribes at home traction, and recommends I not use the arm levers on the Schwinn Airdyne bike. Irv seems unconcerned and tells me he's too busy to travel four hours round trip to do exercise cycles with me on Long Island. Although Michele continues to work with me, I call Irv and insist he come out to see me. When he arrives, I express my anger about his lack of attention, which resulted in my orthopedic problems. When I tell Irv that I expect to see him once a week, he promises to come to the house every Thursday or Friday.

But he does not return for two weeks. He is always saying the National Institutes of Health (NIH) or Walter Reed Army Medical Center in the Baltimore-Washington area are calling him to lecture on his SRWE program, which they want to start using there as a treatment for people with chronic illness. In all, I see Irv only two more times during the remaining seven weeks on Long Island.

Much as I love my family, after five months in New York I want to return to Orlando. I miss my dogs, whom I left at home with Brian, and the accessibility of my house, which means independence.

With Irv's approval, I make plans to return to Orlando in November. He promises to be there the day after I arrive, assures me that he will visit periodically, talk with me daily, and hire a local physical therapist to work with me. I recommend Bob Kogut, particularly talented and sensitive; someone who has lived inside the body of a disabled person. Twenty-five years ago he was in a motorcycle accident that put him in a coma for several weeks. No one believed that he would live, and when he emerged from the coma the doctors said he would never walk again. Again, this was incorrect. When Bob recovered, he quit his job as a factory worker to train as a physical therapist. Somehow, I feel a strong connection to him.

I leave New York on Friday, November 1, 1991, and stop in Pittsburgh for two days to attend my twenty-five-year class reunion at Carnegie-Mellon University.

Members of the Alumni Committee who saw the *People* article have asked me to be the guest speaker and Saturday morning I talk about the past:

> I was thinking about the advantages of being a student here in the sixties. There were enormously talented and creative people in our classes.
>
> There was no cable TV or Nintendo . . . We read books. We didn't watch music . . . We listened to it.
>
> We didn't know we were yuppies in training. Status was not defined by designer initials on our clothing . . . We wore sweatshirts and jeans without labels. We believed in justice, in truth, in the power of words and the need for knowledge.
>
> In the past twenty-five years, I've learned that we make a living by what we do but we make a life by what we give . . .

Most of my college friends do not know about my MS and to my delight, it does not invade our reunion. My five closest friends come to my hotel room with a yearbook and we reminisce for hours. Our friendships have endured and we easily resume conversations that began twenty-five years ago.

It's a terrific weekend and we plan to get together again for a fifty-year class reunion in 2016.

Part III

*The only thing necessary for the triumph
of evil is for good men to do nothing.*
        —*Attributed to Edmund Burke*

CHAPTER 12

Just a Temporary Setback

Fall/Winter 1991

Irv insists that I am not strong enough to return to work so I apply for Social Security disability and file for disability payments with the company that insures the on-air talent and management at the TV station. Although I won't do any reporting, I will appear as a guest on the noon news once a week and answer phone calls from consumers.

I am back home Sunday evening, November 3, 1991, and Irv is supposed to arrive in Orlando the following day. Instead, he calls to say he has to first meet with computer programmers at the University of Pittsburgh and will arrive Thursday. He doesn't get there until Friday, November 8, the day before the Ellen MacFarlane Walk for MS.

Patricia, who is staying with me, comes to the airport with me to meet Irv's plane. I insist on driving my van but my hands are now so weak that she has to maneuver the steering wheel when I switch lanes.

Irv, over six feet tall, looking fit, albeit with a slight roll of flesh around the beltline and with wavy gray hair, is easy to spot in a crowd. He is wearing his trademark outfit—beige trousers, a sweatshirt, and running shoes—and has a satchel slung over his shoulder. He's a day late, he says, because there were storms in Pittsburgh and he doesn't feel comfortable flying in bad weather.

"Do you want me to collect your bags," Patricia asks, "so you and Ellen can go directly to the van?" Fixing his eyes on the ground and walking briskly at the side of my scooter, Irv taps his satchel: "This is it."

"So, how you doing?" Irv asks me with a smile. I tell him the heart rate numbers I've had the last two days.

"Good," he says. "You're doing well. Now, if we can just get the numbers to make bigger swings. That's what we want to get at."

He tells me about the progress of another MS patient with such excitement that we almost pass my van in the parking lot. "She [the patient] walked up a flight of stairs," he says, "after she was outside in the hot sun for a half hour. It's incredible!"

It's always reassuring when he tells me about other patients who are doing well. At least with me, he doesn't subscribe to the notion of doctor-patient confidentiality. He tells me almost everything about everyone. In fact, he even encourages patients to talk to each other by phone and, if possible, in person. This way patients might not feel so alone or become discouraged during down periods.

Just before I left New York, for example, Irv enlisted me to give a pep talk to a physician with MS who was losing faith in Irv's program and was about to quit.

One of the things I really like about Irv is the casual relationships he forges with his patients. I've shared a lot of intimate thoughts with him, telling him about my life, including details about my failed suicide. Irv encourages this communication because he believes every illness has an emotional underpinning that creates waves.

I ask Irv if he would like to stop at his hotel to unpack. He says it isn't necessary: "I'd rather get started immediately on the exercise cycles."

When I mention that Bob, the physical therapist I thought he was going to hire, had to go out of town at the last minute but will be back on Monday, Irv shrugs and says, "Fine, I'll see him then or on my next visit." Had Irv arrived yesterday, when he was expected, Bob would have been here.

At the house, after he looks at and approves the equipment in my gym, Irv leads me through a few exercise cycles. While I recover, he gives me heart rate numbers to try to reach in the afternoon and then my housekeeper, Vicky, drives Irv to his hotel.

On his way out the door, he arranges to meet me the next morning to attend the walk and says he is looking forward to this event. So am I because some of my colleagues, whom I've told about his program, are eager to meet Irv. Somehow Irv's presence at the walk will make my impending recovery more real to them.

Brian, who has not yet moved out of my house and is staying with a friend while Patricia is here, will be driving us to the MS walk.

At the walk Irv is quiet, standing off to the side on the grass, explaining his theory to the news director at my station.

This is the first year I will not be able to walk with the other competitors. Instead, I sit in my scooter, give a pep talk, and cut the ribbon to start the race.

However, I tell a reporter from my TV station who interviews me that, thanks to Irv, I not only will be returning to work full-time in the near future, but will be at the head of the line at next year's walk.

Afterward, we return to my house and Irv guides me through some exercise cycles. The workout lasts under an hour, which is all the time Irv says he can afford because, he suddenly announces, he must leave for the airport for his flight home. I am really surprised because I understood that Irv would stay for about a week to work with me and to train Bob or another physical therapist.

Before I can protest, Irv says that since I have fully mastered his regimen, I am perfectly capable of doing it all on my own. Besides, he is going to send Michele to Orlando to monitor my progress. I am hugely disappointed.

Brian, who arrives at the house later in the day, asks, "Is Vardik still here?"

"It's Dardik," I correct, "and he had to leave."

"Dardik, Vardik, whatever," is all Brian says about him. And Patricia, who I later find out was quite vexed by Irv's hasty departure, has no comment.

A few weeks after Irv's departure, I am the keynote speaker for the National Multiple Sclerosis Society Conference on Employment and MS:

> When I was first diagnosed in 1986, I told my employer, Mike Schweitzer, general manager of WCPX-TV, that although MS has the prognosis of a question mark, I would not let it stop me and that I would do as much work as possible with the limitations it might impose. On good days, I would be more productive to make up for the bad times.
>
> In 1990, when the MS took a severe chronic progressive course, Mike helped me to accommodate the changes by adding staff to my unit and moving me into an office that had a separate temperature control and was close to a bathroom. I could not have remained productive without his support, generosity, and sensitivity.
>
> If not for my employer, I might have lost my will to move on, and the TV station would have lost a productive employee . . .
>
> You all are often the first ones called when there's a diagnosis of MS so it's critical that you motivate instead of console. You need to tell them what they can do, not what they can't do, and help them set realistic goals.
>
> I would urge you to urge employers to give us a chance . . . to recognize that the real disability is an incapacity to notice the person, instead of the limp, or cane or wheelchair.

Later that day, Daniel J. Travanti, from the hit TV series "Hill

"The twins," Ellen (left) and Patricia, four years of age, summer 1949.

LEFT TO RIGHT: Karen (in chair), Ellen (petting kitten), Judd on Mommy's lap, Mommy, Patricia, Jessica; John in front, 1955, in a photo taken for Mother's first campaign for Children's Court Judge. Ellen was ten then.

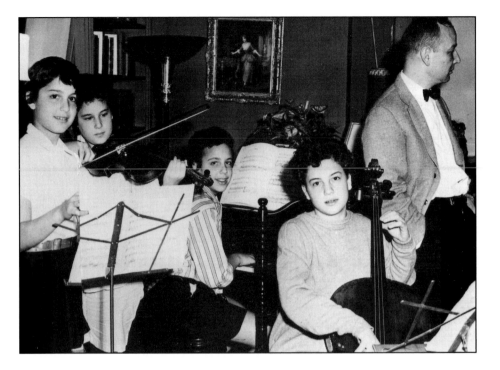

ABOVE: Father's Day, 1959, when we performed a Haydn trio as a present: Ellen on violin, Karen on cello, and Patricia on piano—with Jessica as page-turner and our father listening. Ellen was fourteen then.

LEFT: Ellen, a chubby fifteen-year-old in a high school photo, 1960.

Ellen, New York City, 1973.
Photo by Jessica Burstein

Promotion for Ellen's 1975 TV news series on how to stop
smoking. She quit cold turkey after her father's
lung cancer diagnosis in 1983.
Photo courtesy of KGTV, San Diego

Brian and Ellen at a movie screening in New York City in
January 1981, within a month after marrying.
Photo by Paul Schumach

Promotion shot of Ellen as
Channel 9 reporter, 1984.
Photo courtesy of WFTV, Orlando

Promotion shot of
Ellen as Action 6 TV
investigative consumer
reporter, 1986.
Photo courtesy of WCPX-TV

Ellen on the lecture circuit as a crusading TV reporter,
in Orlando, Florida, winter 1986.

Ellen in WCPX-TV news van, 1987.

Ellen with Brian (left) and brother John at the Ellen MacFarlane
Walk for MS, November 1988.

THE ORLANDO SENTINEL • OCTOBER 21, 1990

Florida

ELLEN MacFARLANE
COMING AT YOU

•

Nothing stops this consumer reporter
in her quest to ambush creeps
and swindlers – not threats,
not slammed doors,
not even multiple sclerosis

PLUS : FUNNY FACES AND DRIVER LICENSES

An October 1990 *Florida* magazine cover photo of Ellen and her cameraman,
R. C. Lee, was taken soon after Ellen went through chemotheraphy and lost her hair.
Photo by Bobby Coker/ORLANDO SENTINEL

LEFT: Ellen ("I love the sound of the engine cranking up") in her motorized scooter, her new mode of legwork, April 1991.
Photo courtesy of WCPX-TV

BELOW: Ellen and her cameraman R.C. ("I'll take care of you, babe," he says . . . he always does), April 1991.
Photo courtesy of WCPX-TV

"I don't change what I do—just the way I do it." Ellen,
en route to cover a story, April 1991.
Photo courtesy of WCPX-TV

Ellen, at home, working with customized RGO braces, April 1993.
Photo by Patricia Burstein

Ellen at work on the book at her computer, November 1993.
Photo by Patricia Burstein

Butter, taking a break from working on *Legwork*, September 1993.
Photo by Patricia Burstein

Ellen and her canine companion and best buddy, Butter, November 1993.
Photo by Jacque Wishon

Ellen in her scooter.
Photo by Jessica Burstein

Street Blues," whose brother has MS, tapes a public information spot featuring me as part of the National Multiple Sclerosis Society campaign on employment.

At home, Michele calls me daily to give me target heart rate (HR) numbers. I send the results every evening by computer:

START TIME: 7:50 A.M.

TARGET	START HR	HIGH HR
E	70	81
E	71	81
E	70	86
10 MIN. NAP		
110	69	111
117	67	121
120	69	122
124	68	123

START TIME: 9:05 A.M.

TARGET	START HR	HIGH HR
120	70	120
136	72	135
145	77	144
110	82	112

START TIME: 11 A.M.

TARGET	START HR	HIGH HR
E	68	78
E	67	80
125	73	127
150	72	148
10 MIN.		
135	70	137
E	71	84
E	70	86

START TIME: 2:30 P.M.

TARGET	START HR	HIGH HR
E	85	106
100	83	107
117	81	123
127	82	129

START TIME: 4:30 P.M.

TARGET	START HR	HIGH HR
E	83	94
152	84	147
130	90	133

I also answer a questionnaire every evening:

1. Your overall energy level at 7 A.M. was: (1=low, 10=high)
2. Your overall energy level at 10 A.M. was: (1=low, 10=high)
3. Your overall energy level at 2 P.M. was: (1=low, 10=high)
4. Your overall energy level at 4 P.M. was: (1=low, 10=high)
5. Your overall energy level at 8 P.M. was: (1=low, 10=high)
6. Your balance this morning was: (1=bad, 10=good)
7. Your balance this afternoon was: (1=bad, 10=good)
8. Your balance this evening was: (1=bad, 10=good)
9. Numbness in your arms? (R=Right, L=Left, B=Both, N=None)
10. Numbness in your legs? (R=Right, L=Left, B=Both, N=None)
11. Rate your mental alertness for today: (1=low, 10=high)
12. Rate your level of anxiety for today: (1=low, 10=high)
13. Rate your level of depression for today: (1=low, 10=high)
14. Rate your level of anger for today: (1=low, 10=high)
15. Rate your mood for today: (1=bad, 10=good)
16. Rate your confidence level for today: (1=bad, 10=good)
17. What time did you go to bed last night? (24-hr. time)
18. How many hours did you actually sleep? (24-hr. time)
19. What was your quality of sleep? (1=low, 10=high)

20. What time did you nap today? (24-hr. time, 00:00=no nap)
21. How long did you nap today? (24-hr. time, 00:00=no nap)
22. How was your bladder function? (1=bad, 10=good)
23. Did you have excess exposure to heat? (Y=Yes, N=No)
24. Your limbs felt: (1=cold, 10=hot)
25. Did you take hot/cold showers: (A=A.M., P=P.M., B=Both, N=None)

Michele comes to Orlando to work with me for two days in December, and after she leaves, I get a bill from Irv. He wants me to pay over fifteen hundred dollars for his hotel and airfare and Michele's airfare.

Greatly upset, I call my mother, who tells me that she had written to Irv, prior to my leaving New York, to express her concern about his increasing lack of attention to my case. Worried about disrupting my relationship with Irv, she tempered the letter and asked him not to discuss it with me.

Irv ignores my mother's request that he call to discuss her concerns. Instead, he waits a month, until after I return to Orlando, to send her a letter.

I ask my mother to fax me both her letter and Irv's response.

September 27, 1991

Dear Dr. Dardik:

I am writing to you now, because this is the third to last payment due under our agreement, and I do not want to let the occasion pass without expressing my serious concerns about the intermittent nature of your personal contact with Ellen.

. . . Let me be very clear. The money is not at issue. I would pay anything to make my daughter feel better . . . You made a promise to a very ill woman that she would have this attention, presence and observation on a regular basis. This is not a promise it is either fair or honorable to break . . .

. . . Apart from the fact that you have contracted to do this, you are, it seems to me, obligated to be there for her by the con-

151

cern and interest and commitment you expressed to her when treatment began . . .

> Sincerely yours,
> Beatrice S. Burstein

<hr>

October 25, 1991

Dear Judge Burstein:

. . . I pointed out that my principal objective was to use the program to get Ellen on her own two feet. I indicated that my approach to the treatment of her problem was somewhat unique and that it would be best to do it "my way . . ."

> Very truly yours,
> Irving I. Dardik

Irv's letter also contains several lies that infuriate me. For example: "I speak with Ellen 4 or 5 times a week, often in the presence of the therapist"; "While Ellen was in Manhattan, I visited her approximately two to three times a week in the beginning and then reduced the frequency of visits to once every week"; "In Long Island, I visited Ellen five out of six weeks."

I send Irv a letter:

December 3, 1991

Dear Irv:

. . . While I don't want to get involved in a "he says" "she says" argument, I must take issue with a number of claims you made in your letter to my mother . . .

I have great concern that you would seek to charge me for expenses that were never part of our agreement. I understood that the 100 thousand dollars for a year's treatment with lifetime follow-up would cover Michele's visits to me, almost daily in New York or monthly in Orlando. After all, I moved from New York City to Long Island and then to Orlando only after consulting with you and with your approval. Moreover, you were originally going to hire a therapist to work with me in Orlando at no additional cost to me . . .

I believe in paying my bills, but I also believe in being fair. I have enormous respect, admiration, and affection for you and I do not want a dispute over money to jeopardize our relationship and sabotage my recovery. I hope we can resolve this.

Please call after you've had a chance to review my comments.

Sincerely,

Ellen Burstein MacFarlane

Irv doesn't call, although according to Michele, he received my letter. But in our next conversation, Irv mentions that he may have a new patient and part of the fee from that person will cover visits to me.

Michele returns in January for another few days, and I am able to get my heart rate above 160 two days in a row. Then, I experience what appears to be a miracle. Unassisted, without my walker or braces, I am able to walk the entire length of my house, thirty-three hundred square feet.

"Incredible!" Irv yells when we call him. "Remember when I told you, Ellen, that you would walk when your heart rate reaches 160? I'm going to send Michele to Orlando every other week!"

But Michele doesn't return for six weeks. The miracle never repeats itself and within days of Michele's leaving, I begin to lose strength. When I try to reach Irv by phone, he is never available. Eventually, I get his wife, Alison, who puts him on the line.

"Don't worry, Ellen," Irv says. "It's an expected decline. You'll come back soon—stronger than ever." But I don't.

By March I am worse than I've even been since I got MS. After leaving dozens of messages for Irv, I finally get him on the phone. This time he recommends that I return to New York so he, personally, can bring me out of this downward spiral.

With only three months left in the program, I cannot afford not to believe him.

CHAPTER 13

The Light
Is Out

Spring 1992

S orry, Mom, my scooter just crashed into the wall."
"Don't worry," she says. "It's not important."

Once again I am back in New York staying at our family home. It is a rambling Dutch Colonial house with all our bedrooms preserved, just as my late father wanted. But he had six able-bodied children then and—save for the electric seatlift my mother has installed—the house is not handicapped-accessible. I am staying in a bedroom on the second floor and my scooter is destroying the narrow hallways.

But it is comforting to be with my family, and Irv, as promised, will turn up and cure me. Then, I can walk up and down staircases and slide down banisters, just as I did when I was a little girl in my pajamas, grabbing desserts on the run at my parents' dinner parties.

Only this time I won't be going to a party, but more like a funeral for my MS. Irv, who still claims he can cure me, is a no-show, not even calling me or surfacing to examine or evaluate my deterioration.

Instead, he sends various employees, including the newest member of his team, a sociologist, to lead me through exercise cycles. And it is this same sociologist who answers all my questions now.

I just feel rotten. I need Irv to explain my deterioration: the overwhelming exhaustion, muscle contractions, and loss of strength. I can no longer raise my arms above my head or use my right hand. Worst of all, the bladder incontinence problem I developed after chemotherapy is now so severe that I have to wear diapers all the time. Even if I could walk, I couldn't get to the bathroom in time to use the toilet.

I'm on the toilet so frequently and use so many diapers that my mother and Jessica suggest that I might have more freedom if I catheterize myself.

Just the thought of this scares me more than anything else about MS; especially because my hands aren't strong or flexible enough to do it myself and I would need a nurse to insert the catheters. And I am also concerned about infections that frequently result from catheterization.

Jessica, who cannot bear to see me suffer any discomfort, convinces me to at least consult a urologist. I give in and, fortunately, a catheter isn't necessary. The urologist thinks I'll do better with medication. The pills are somewhat helpful and I decide to go to a bladder clinic when I return to Orlando.

After my visit to the urologist, I tell my mother and Jessica that while I appreciate their concern and their desire to ease my pain, I am not a child and I am perfectly capable of making decisions about my health. I can't convince my family to stop telling me what I feel or to believe that I say exactly what I mean and will ask for help when I need it.

One night in April, I have a dream where I am walking and jumping up and down and for the first time since I've had MS I have no pain and my body feels normal. When Linda Podhurst, the sociologist and the newest addition to Irv's staff, calls me the next day, I tell her about the dream.

"Also, Linda, I just zipped through the cycles today," I report. "I shut down only two times—at two o'clock and 5:15 P.M."

"Do you lay [*sic*] down then?"

"No," I tell her, "Michele said not to get into bed until nine-thirty."

"What does she want you to do in the evenings? Just kind of sit up?"

Linda, who says she has an M.A. from Rutgers University in sociology—with a specialty in alternative medicine—is encouraging me to speak to the spiritual side of myself again. This last year, believing Irv's promise to cure me, I stopped my daily practice of meditating and visualizing. It was a mistake, and now I am, once again, developing my interior self.

When I tell Linda that I no longer identify with the MS, she says, "That's great . . . And you save so much energy not addressing it. Yeah, it's like you cut yourself off from it . . . So, what kind of cycles does Michele have you on tomorrow?"

"I'm supposed to do thirty cycles tomorrow. All easies," which are exercises requiring minor efforts like standing and sitting down. "And by Monday I'll go back to the heavy cycles—if I'm able to get on the Schwinn Airdyne bike."

I don't get back on the bike because, by Sunday, I have severe pain again in my shoulder, neck, and back. When I call Irv on Monday, the secretary tells me that he's not well; while lifting a couch, he hurt his back and is at the chiropractor's office.

And although my aide, Mary Ann, has recovered from her appendectomy, she is also in no condition to help. She is in the middle of a divorce. Confused and upset about her life, she has become a woman in search of a disease. I never know what to expect. Today it's her stomach; yesterday it was her ovaries; tomorrow it could be her toes or, as Patricia puts it, "a hole in her head." Still, she is very good-natured.

While Mary Ann undergoes medical tests for her unknown condition, a home aide, Ramona Lattimore, a fortyish woman with lovely, soft hands and a bright, amusing mind, looks after me. She gets me up in the morning, takes care of me during the day, and at night, whoever is in the house, usually Patricia or Jessica, helps me get into bed.

Meanwhile, Irv's therapists continue to turn up at the house to supervise exercise cycles, most of which I can no longer do. They're so inexperienced that one of them fails to notice, after slight exercise, that my heart rate plummets to the low 40s. This makes me wonder if maybe all along I've been feeding my heart rate numbers into the wind rather than into a computer.

You do not know your hope is gone until you look for it and it is no longer there. I wake this morning in early May with dread. For weeks now, I have been putting off a visit to Dr. Weinreb, who wants to check how I'm doing on the 4-AP. All along, I have been waiting for a good day to come along to see him. That way, I might be able to fool him—and myself—into thinking I am better.

Like other MS patients, I can sometimes succeed at this self-deception because of the disease's unpredictable nature. There are months of quiescence interrupted by debilitating exacerbations that leave behind what doctors call deficits.

To me they are losses, immeasurable and inconsolable. I tell no one that for many months my reading has been confined to audio cassettes, not by choice, but because my hands are too weak to hold a book or turn pages. With my form of MS, severe chronic progressive, there are few good days left anymore. Getting better means not getting worse.

Anyhow, this clearly is not a good day. I am extremely fatigued and weak. My hands are ice-cold and my legs, which feel as if they were shot with Novocain, refuse to support me. And my aide, Ramona, is finding it difficult to keep my contracted body upright in order to lift me out of bed and into my scooter.

At six o'clock in the morning I start to get ready for my ten o'clock appointment with Dr. Weinreb in the city. It takes an hour by car from our family home on Long Island to his office, which leaves me three hours for Ramona to stretch my legs, get me on the toilet, fasten my diaper, wash my face, help me brush my teeth, dress, and feed me. Then I must be transported by chairlift to the ground floor.

After switching to another scooter, I travel over two ramps to reach the driveway and, finally, the car. From bedroom to car takes a half hour. My sisters help me. The scooter must first be disassembled to fit into the trunk of the car so Patricia recommends, "Let's use the wheelchair instead of the scooter today."

I insist that I do not need either one. That I am mobile enough to rely on the walker to cross the twenty yards from the lobby to the elevator and then along a corridor to Weinreb's office. Whether or not they believe this, at least they do not challenge me and I am grateful. Though I am in a down period, I want to believe what Irv has repeatedly told me: it is temporary and I will bounce back and be stronger for it. Yet how much longer can I keep telling myself stories about his miracle cure? I just need someone, anyone, to say it will come true.

For the moment I am not even experiencing a placebo effect. It is ten minutes since I arrived at the New York University Medical Center and, forget the walker, I am still trying to get out of the car. The driver and my sisters hoist me out of it and into a wheelchair they retrieved from the lobby. "Oh well," I tell them, "just till I get upstairs. Then I'll transfer to the walker."

I arrive at Dr. Herman Weinreb's office in a wheelchair, after all. "Hi," he greets me. "It is good to see you again. How are you doing?"

"Look," I say, "no braces," something I wore to my appointment a year ago.

"Good," he mumbles. But I am sure he is thinking: *But you need your sisters to keep you upright.*

They are trying to lift me up and hoist me onto the examining table. It is no use. I am too weak and fall back into the wheelchair.

I fasten my hope now on another Irv patient, Tracey.

"Irv is also working with her," I report. "He says you are impressed by how well she is doing in the program."

"No she's not," Weinreb grumbles. "She went back to Ohio. The program is just an exorbitantly priced exercise routine."

As Weinreb examines me, I point out that my feet are no longer numb, my legs are not as stiff, and Lhermitte's sign is gone—the latter an MS sensation that feels like an electrical shock in your neck when you bend your head.

There's also no evidence of Babinski's sign, yet another symptom, where the toes curl under when you touch the soles of the feet. I want Weinreb to acknowledge the benefits of Irv's program. But he has an altogether different explanation:

"We are finding the 4-AP increases mobility and energy, improves the eyesight, and reduces spasticity." When I tell him that, in January, I walked the length of my house, Weinreb says, again, "That's the 4-AP." All I want is his reassurance about Irv, but it is not forthcoming.

Weinreb looks pained and as we say good-bye all he can come up with is, "You're about the same as you were a year ago."

I do not want to talk or even think about Irv. Until now, I have been buoyed by the hope this man would cure me, and I am unwilling to yield to my growing suspicions about him.

On the ride home Patricia tries to fill the dark hole of silence. "Weinreb is a decent man," she comments. "He really cares about you."

"That may be true," I say, "but I still have MS."

Whenever my condition becomes unbearable, I can always find something to draw on. Now, for example, I tell myself, *Look, it could be worse—I could be all alone in the world with no family to care about me and to help support me financially.* At the same time, I worry about the cost of my illness, in particular the one hundred thousand dollars Irv got, and with my father dead almost nine years, how my family can continue to absorb this.

Immediately, I latch onto another positive: at least with my disability insurance payments I can support the upkeep of my home in Orlando on my own. There, I am recognized for my professional achievements, not for being the reporter who has MS. It is difficult enough to witness my life becoming unraveled by MS without also having to uproot myself.

None of the above, though, is enough. At least, before today, I could convince myself, *Well, I'll get up and around when I'm better.* But I now know that I am not getting better and I'll probably get worse. Will people still want to be around me? And how do I establish relationships when I never know from one hour to the next how I am going to be feeling?

I know that Weinreb's statement, that my condition is the same, can't be true. He's only trying to be kind when he says this. A year ago I used the walker to reach his office and got on the examining table with minimal assistance.

Once I arrive at the house, from car to bedroom takes me forty-five minutes. My mother is waiting for me. "How did it go?" she inquires.

"Fine," I say. "There's less spasticity . . . I'm about the same as a year ago." I know she hears the heartache in my voice. But there are no answers to my agony and there is nothing to say.

Ramona brings me lunch, but I have no appetite. I sit alone in my room, right below my childhood bedroom, which I would like to visit again, but cannot climb the flight of stairs to reach. I feel imprisoned in my body with my mind on watch, like a sentry, looking for any sign of well-being—any sign of movement, anything, in my arms or legs. I am stuck.

I am also devastated because my dog, Churchill, is very ill and I am too weak to travel to Orlando to comfort him. He has cataracts in both eyes and the corneas are so inflamed that the vet may have to remove one or both of his eyes.

When I fall on the floor and sob, "Please let me up . . . let me out of this body," Churchill never fails to rescue me from my sorrow. He does not see a disability, only a playmate to whom he brings his ball. But I am sure that, consistent as Churchill has been in his devotion to me all these years, he cannot understand why I am not there when he needs me.

Two months remain in Irv's program. But I am not sure I have the inner strength or belief anymore that eventually he will cure me. I press the speaker button on my phone, which I am too weak to lift or hold, to call him. I get his answering machine.

"I saw Dr. Weinreb today," I report, "and he says, except for less spasticity, I am not any better than last year. The 4-AP is the only reason for any improvement. Please give me a call. I need you to explain what is happening to me."

Minutes later, Michele calls back and reports, "Irv is so upset."

I am incredulous: "What's he so upset about—I'm the one with the MS."

My calm voice belies my despair and growing anger. I do not want to jinx the positive spin, no doubt, he will put on my predicament. I am fighting for my life.

Only today is not just a battle. It is a war and I am losing it. I am totally devastated. I have worked so hard to beat the MS and come so far, only to find out these ten months have been useless. All I did was give up a little more of myself, fighting it, trying to stay on my feet.

I now know there is nothing I can do anymore to change the outcome. I have no hope of ever walking again. I go inside myself to look for the light that has always given me the strength and the will to keep going.

This time I find the light is out.

CHAPTER 14

I Don't Have to Take This

Early August 1992

For the first time in more than eight months I am seeing Irv. But he does not come to me. I must go to him. I now know he is a liar and a cheat, but I agree to do so because I am someone who believes that every experience must have a beginning, a middle, and an end. However, the MS, unfortunately, does not yield to my thinking—the agony of it is never-ending.

"Irv's Camp," as Michele calls his place, is actually an eighty-five-acre farm in New Jersey, with horses his wife, Alison, breeds. The set-up is a surprise because, according to the magazine article, where I and many other patients first came to know about Irv, he was said to be near bankruptcy from both an alimony war with his ex-wife and the cost of researching his brainstorms.

Only Irv's favorite patients, according to Michele, are invited here. However, a more likely explanation may be that Irv is avoiding my mother's repeated requests that he come to our home to speak with her. The news of the 4-AP, not Irv, being responsible for any slight improvement in my otherwise debilitating condition further unsettles him.

Though the yearlong program ended officially for me a month ago, Irv has yet to figure out a way to bring it to a close without injury to himself. Both the health reporter at my TV station and the local newspaper are eager to follow up on my progress upon my return to Orlando.

Still, Irv banks on patients, already diminished by their illness, being reluctant to admit publicly that they have been conned.

Anyway, upon arriving at "Irv's Camp" around one o'clock in the afternoon on this day in early August, Irv's secretary directs me and my aide, Mary Ann, to the cottage. And, once again, Irv is a no-show. Although there is a ramp leading up to the cottage porch, once inside I can't get to the bathroom because the doorway is too narrow for my scooter.

And the cottage is filthy and there is nothing—not even a carton of juice or can of soda—in the refrigerator.

In the mess, which Mary Ann starts to clean up, I find a list of Irv's patients and copies of the *New York* magazine cover story on him. How I wish that article had appeared instead in the *National Enquirer* because then I would not have seen it and I wouldn't be here now.

My experiences with Irv seem like the plot of a novel that might be titled *Anatomy of a Con.* Except this is happening to me and it isn't fiction.

For the next five and a half hours—still no Irv. I wait for him to call to explain his absence at the very least. He doesn't. Fortunately, I brought my laptop computer and with the only two fingers that still function I type a list of Irv's patients.

At 6:30 P.M., entirely fed up, exhausted, and hungry, I call my mother to say I want to leave. She calls Irv, gets his answering machine, and leaves a message saying she is appalled by this, his latest, indecency. Only then, five minutes later, does he turn up at the cottage.

I tell him that I've had enough, that I'm wasting my time, and that I'm leaving. This is the first time I am able to express my anger.

As he stands on the porch Irv looks at me with dead eyes and says, "I don't have to take this."

His wife, Alison, arrives, apologizes for Irv's outburst, pleads with me not to leave, and invites me and Mary Ann to dinner. Ultimately, they have to bring dinner to me because it's pouring and my scooter can't travel over the dirt road, now a huge mud puddle, to their house.

Despite my fury, I decide to stay after all. I call my mother and for the first time she says what she has been thinking all along—I have been fooling myself about Irv. I tell her I agree, but I'm staying to give Irv a final chance to work his supposed miracle on me, and to preempt him from ever saying in the future that I did not give him every chance to cure me. Besides, I am too exhausted to ride in a car for two hours for a second time today.

Irv and Alison bring us dinner and this time Alison apologizes for Irv's no-show all day. Their explanation: a priest who was setting up an alternative medicine seminar was leaving that day for Rio de Janeiro and they had to meet him at the airport prior to his flight.

I stay five days during which Irv works with me for less than five hours. Whenever he bothers to show up and I am not too weak, he leads me through a few easy exercise cycles on a Schwinn Airdyne bike in the cottage and on equipment in his barn.

During my recovery periods, he reiterates the same litany about how effective his program is and how it will cure me. Two nights later, when Irv and Alison leave, Mary Ann and I are all alone on the property and I just pray, with all the stress, I don't need a doctor.

In his absence, Michele shows up twice, also to lead me through a few cycles and to give me a few pep talks and tell me how lucky I am to be working with Irv. Neither Irv, nor Alison, nor Michele is aware that I am finished with him and his SRWE program. On the day of departure, I make sure to pack the computer disk with the file containing the list of Irv's patients. It may just come in handy.

When I return to my family home there are two messages for me from two of Irv's prospective patients. One is an engineer whom Irv wants to charge a thousand dollars for a consultation and who is also expected to travel from the Washington, D.C., area to "Irv's Camp" for this. And there is a young woman whose parents have to take out a second mortgage to afford Irv's program. As it is, they can't even pay for private-duty nurses if she decides to undergo Cytoxan chemotherapy, as recommended by her neurologist.

Because I previously endorsed Irv when people called me, I feel horribly guilty. As difficult as it will be for me to admit publicly that he cheated me, now that I know, I must tell people.

This, after all, is what I did for a living before I met Irv, the cruelest charlatan of all. This time, it's not a story about a used car. It's about my and others' desperation to get well.

———

It is noon on a day in late August and I am in Labe's office for the first time in fifteen months. Usually I see him three or four times a year. But once Irv promised I would be walking within a year, I vanished inside my own wishful thinking.

It is one thing to suspect you may be getting worse; quite another to believe or to confirm it. I avoided Labe because I did not want any bad news.

Today it is worse than bad. It is crushing.

"How much time do I have left?" I ask Labe.

"If the progression doesn't stop, we're looking at quadriplegic within three years."

I know Labe is heartbroken about my rapid decline this last year. And he is enraged by what I tell him about Irv's false promises, truancies, and greed.

At this moment, I begin to really grieve for the year Irv took that I could not afford to lose. Maybe I was buying "hope" but, sorrowfully, the underbelly of the "hope" Irv sells is only wretched despair.

And the agony my family also endured watching me deteriorate!

But, again, what other option was there? All along, as one after the other of Irv's promises slipped away, I kept having to adjust my expectations. To surrender my belief in Irv would have meant giving up hope. There wasn't even a chance for a placebo effect either, because Irv just wasn't there for the so-called laying on of the hands by healers.

Had he acted in good faith and honored his commitment to work one-on-one with me, then I would have said to myself, "Okay, he tried his best but it just didn't work." But he didn't.

Labe and I spend the better part of the afternoon talking. To try to slow the progression Labe says he is putting me back on the Imuran.

What, I ask Labe, is left of my life? I know now that unless someone comes up with a cure for MS, I will never walk, jog, or dance again. Even with a cure, there may be no way to recapture the function I have already lost. Though I do not believe in suicide anymore, I still feel as though I want to die.

My work, so important to me and which upon Irv's instructions I put on hold, is now gone—except for the possibility of a consumer call-in segment.

Labe manages somehow to move me past my misery and into other areas of mutual interest: books, presidential politics, and travel.

Before we say good-bye, Labe writes three prescriptions for me. One is for Imuran; another for a full-time aide, which, he says, can make the difference between being an invalid and being disabled. Labe also reminds me that a disability did not stop FDR from being President. Paralyzed from polio, he needed aides to help him physically so he would have enough energy to run the country.

The third prescription reads, simply: "Find a passion in your life."

———

For weeks my family, knowing I am returning shortly to Orlando, echoes Labe's thinking about an aide. I resist. It is a particularly painful issue for me. It means yet another loss of my independence and a further erosion of my self-esteem. Allowing a complete stranger into my life to perform intimate tasks, like bathing and dressing me, is also awkward, if not a bit scary. Always, this relationship is a struggle. On some level, though, I am fooling myself. At the family house an aide looks after me during the day, and at night the household help and my siblings pitch in. Someone is always there.

At home in Orlando, my housekeeper, Vicky, has managed over the last year to move into the role of caretaker, bathing, dressing, and feeding me, without calling attention to it. At night, after she helps me into bed, I rely on a medical alert and alarm system.

Vicky wears regular, civilian, clothes. Whomever I hire—if and when I should decide to fill Labe's prescription—must dress similarly. A nurse's uniform would only be still another reminder of my MS.

At some level we are all vulnerable. Even I, as an investigative consumer journalist, the least likely to be taken, got conned. And this time the MS has scored its greatest victory. It made me so desperate that I believed Dr. Irving I. Dardik's lies and allowed him to take my family's money and destroy my hope.

———

It is September 1, 1992, and I am getting worse: I cannot lift my arms to drink from a glass, brush my teeth, wash my face and body, comb my hair, apply makeup, blow my nose, or even scratch an itch.

It would be unforgivable for me to ignore what Irv has done. I cannot let him cheat other chronically ill people, particularly those with limited resources. Any discomfort I may feel about going public is outweighed by my desire to stop him from damaging anyone else. This is consistent with who I am and what I do.

So how do I begin again? First, I tell the truth.

———

Over Labor Day weekend I fax Irv a letter:

September 3, 1992

Dear Irv:

When I met you in June 1991, after reading the *New York* magazine cover story on your wave theory and successes with MS victims, you enthusiastically told me you had the answer to MS and other chronic and fatal illnesses. You said you were not talking about a remission, you could cure me, it would take a year and I would walk again. Unfortunately, I believed you.

. . . Irv, I want to emphasize this is not about the money. It's about decency, honor and truth. It's about your deception, and greed, about taking advantage of the desperation of people who live with the prognosis of a question mark, about demanding an excessive amount of money up-front for a worthless service you don't provide, about ignoring your clients and their families when there's a problem . . .

. . . Last year, I thought you were giving me back my life. Instead, you took a year I could not afford to lose. I feel great horror, regret and embarrassment about my endorsement of you in an *Orlando Sentinel* article about me that appeared in newspapers around the country. I can't do anything about the people who were taken in as a result, but I intend to retract my statements and file complaints with the AMA and the New Jersey and New York boards of medical examiners. I will do my best to stop you from getting rich by cheating people who would pay any amount of money to regain their health.

Sincerely,
Ellen Burstein (MacFarlane)

Part IV

We will grieve not, rather find
Strength in what remains behind.
  —William Wordsworth

CHAPTER 15

Another Chance

September 1992

It is a glorious day, blue skies and no humidity, with the earth deeply green, and I am being lifted into our swimming pool on a chair my mother installed soon after I returned from "Irv's Camp." My brothers and sisters are taking turns, holding a kickboard for me as I walk the width of the pool. The water keeps me buoyant, making it easier to exercise—still one more regret about being locked indoors all summer by Irv and his program.

My twin is expecting guests and I figure I can stay outside, without tiring, until they arrive so I can say hello. They turn up while I am still in the pool, with my scooter parked by the chairlift. They are Henry and Carol; a *Life* magazine photographer–opera singer and a classical pianist, respectively. Also along are their two musically gifted children. Immediately, I feel so comfortable with them that I think better of going inside.

In fact, I feel as if maybe I have known them my whole life, and for the first time in a year, I find myself peppy enough to stay awake and outside the entire day. I savor every minute of this day, the first time I feel alive and full of possibilities in so long.

I also feel entirely comfortable with myself and when Henry and Carol challenge me to a game of Boggle, a puzzle version of Scrabble with the alphabet letters on cubes, I accept. "If you'll shake the cubes for me," I say, feeling absolutely no need to try to hide my disability, "I'll play."

My team, Henry and I, wins. I think I may be back in the game.

———

A few days later I leave for Los Angeles. There, I am hoping to get customized braces that may help me walk again. A friend who saw the *People* magazine profile on me over a year ago told me about them, and after the misery of the Irv experience, I got in touch with the inventor, British-born engineer Dr. Roy Douglas.

Called Reciprocal Gait Orthosis, the braces are made of aluminum and plastic and weigh only five pounds. Largely intended for patients with spinal cord injuries, the braces have an application as well for people challenged by muscular dystrophy, cerebral palsy, spina bifida, and multiple sclerosis. The braces put knees, hips, and ankles in perfect alignment, ultimately helping you to walk normally. They also have the residual effect of straightening out contractions and keeping internal organs properly positioned.

During our first phone conversation Dr. Roy Douglas says he is sending me a video of an MS patient who, after being wheelchairbound for four years, was able to walk normally with the braces. "When you see it," he remarks, "you'll think I'm a charlatan." Before he hangs up, he tells me, "I promise no miracles."

When I ask him about the cost, he tells me he will check to see if my insurance covers it. As it turns out, the braces, with a price tag of ten thousand dollars, are totally reimbursable—unlike Irv's SRWE program, which no insurance company countenances.

When I meet Roy I am struck by his goodness and decency. His eyes light up and a big smile appears whenever he watches someone get up and walk in the braces.

At seventy-one, Roy could retire but he derives too much pleasure from helping people stand up and walk again. His obvious delight shows in his warm and friendly demeanor. I think he is an angel.

It's extraordinary to see despair turn into joy when paraplegics put on the braces and walk. And I am also encouraged by the multidisciplinary approach. Unlike Irv, who runs around taking money up front for his useless program, before Roy and Dr. Paul Berns, director of the center, will approve the braces for me, I must be examined and approved as a candidate for them by an orthopedist, a neurologist, a physical therapist (Doug Hudgens), and a psychiatrist (Dr. Tommy White).

Initially, the orthopedist thinks my shoulder pain comes from a rotator cuff tear which would require surgery and he sends me to a lab for X rays and an MRI. Fortunately, it does not appear in either and I am given several cortisone injections to reduce inflammation and relieve the pain. I also begin six weeks of physical therapy to repair the injury and to retrieve some of the upper body strength I lost during the past year. And then, Roy is still not sure he can help me because I am so weak and still in pain from Irv's regimen. But after two weeks of intensive physical therapy, finally Roy fits me for my braces.

I am starting to feel like my old self again. After a year of imprisonment in Irv's program, I am seeing friends, including an actress and a producer, the latter whom I once dated, again. My twin, Patricia, who is here to do a magazine interview, helps me get settled in the hotel where I am staying. The Carlyle Inn is fully handicapped-accessed and there is also an al fresco dining area just outside my door.

I rent a lightweight wheelchair that can be folded and packed in the trunk of Patricia's rental car and off we go to Malibu on a Saturday for lunch. This is the first time in over a year that I am by the sea, and as always, I find it restorative.

I begin to realize that everywhere I go, people are wonderful to me and want to help. Some shop owners stop what they're doing to give me directions and walk with me, and others give me gifts.

They frequently take my hand or lean down and kiss the top of my head.

Their response reminds me of one of my favorite books from childhood, *The Giving Tree* by Shel Silverstein. It's about unconditional love and not giving up despite losses. It's a tale about a little boy and a tree that loves him. Through the years the tree gives up every part of itself—its apples, its branches, and its trunk—to make the boy happy. Finally, all that is left of the tree is its stump. At the end of the book the boy, now an old man, tells the tree:

> "I am tired."
> The tree responds: "Come boy, sit down, sit down and rest."
> And the boy did.
> And the tree was happy.

My hard work and Roy's efforts pay off. The only dissonance was a call I got from Michele when I first arrived in Los Angeles. She located me through the message I left on my answering machine.

"Guess what, Ellen," she chirped. "I'm coming to Orlando next week."

I answered: "Guess what, Michele, I won't be there. And tell Irv I'm finished with his program, but I'm not finished with him."

I tell my brother Johnny, who has come to Los Angeles to fly back with me to Orlando, about the conversation, adding, "This time I mean business . . . putting Irv out of business."

CHAPTER 16

You Will Never Do This to Anyone Again

December 1992 to April 1993

By December 1992, after three months of taking the immuno-suppressive drug Imuran, the progression of my MS appears to be slowing down. But the severe tendinitis and pain in my right arm and shoulder caused by Irv's treatment prevent me from using this quiescent period to build strength. If not for this, I would have the arm strength that is necessary for walking in my brace.

Yet, I am willing neither to "go gentle into that good night" nor to allow a crook like Irv to taint my future relationships with medical professionals like Bob, my physical therapist. He won't give up. Five days a week, he stretches my limbs, works with exercises and equipment to improve my balance and strength, and uses parallel bars to help me walk in my braces.

My TV colleagues are also unfailingly kind and helpful. I go to the station once a week to answer consumer calls on the noon news.

During this period, I vacillate in my mind about exposing Irv: any emotional distress can set off an exacerbation; my time and energy are limited and I don't want to waste them on an evil person. Yet I cannot let him continue to rip off people who believe his lies about curing their chronic and fatal illnesses.

I call the New York State and New Jersey Board of Medical Examiners to get a definition of medical misconduct. It includes: guaranteeing that a cure will result from medical services; practicing the profession fraudulently, through gross incompetence or gross negligence; and promoting the sale of services, goods, appliances, or drugs in a manner that exploits the patient.

However, before I file a complaint, I want to do some legwork through the computer. While going through magazine databases, I find an article in the July 1986 *Health* magazine about a mail-order UNIQ Quantum XL pulse (heart) monitor. It sounds suspiciously like what Irv sold me and others:

> Dr. Irving I. Dardik is developing a program for the pulse monitor that will allow you to get personalized coaching at home from a local fitness center. You'll simply provide a printout of your workouts to the center, and they'll respond with a printout giving you advice. The plan eventually is to have you communicate back and forth with the center directly through a computer modem hookup. To buy the UNIQ QUANTUM XL or find out about the Dardik program, write to Quantum Life Systems, Inc., RDI, Box 253, Hillcrest Drive, Great Meadows, NJ 07838. The monitor costs $300, but it's a heart-healthy investment.

I and other Irv victims did not have the option of buying just the three-hundred-dollar deal. By the time we read about him in *New York* magazine, Irv had already increased the price, in cases like mine, to one hundred thousand dollars. And his Quantum Life Systems salesmanship is all the more curious because, according to the article by Tony Schwartz, during this period Irv had "to sit broke in a library," having given up a lucrative surgical practice and the prestigious post of chairman of the U.S. Olympic Committee's Sports Medicine Council, "for several years pursuing a theory of how the universe works"; a circumstance, the author adds, that "only makes him [Irv] more intriguing—at least to me."

A search of U.S. corporations reveals that, in 1987, Irv started another company, Cardiocybernetics, Inc. Through January 1992, he is listed as president, his second wife, Alison, as vice president–secretary.

But in April 1992, Irv is no longer listed as an officer of the corporation. Alison, meanwhile, has enjoyed a spectacular promotion to president, succeeding him, and she appears to be a one-person board member. This change coincides with complaints from patients about not being cured and Irv's absences. Of course, in one way, it makes perfect sense that Alison should assume the presidency of Cardiocybernetics, Inc., because, all along, Irv has preferred that she handle the finances and close the sale with patients.

In further research on Irv's background, I discover other inconsistencies and incorrect information. According to the *New York* magazine story, Irv is engaged in an alimony war with his first wife, who is suing him. Well, if he isn't paying her, why does he "sit broke in a library"? Why not sell off some of his eighty-five-acre farm or one of second wife Alison's horses? Further, how come this "highly respected vascular surgeon," said to be earning vast sums of money prior to quitting to pursue SRWE, did not set aside funds to bankroll his brainstorm?

In a search for newspaper articles about Irv, I find that he did not give up his position as chairman of the U.S. Olympic Committee's Sports Medicine Council, as stated in *New York*.

An April 11, 1985, article from the *Los Angeles Times* wire service roundup reads:

> Dr. Irving Dardik has been replaced as Chairman of the United States Olympic Committee's Sports Medicine Council . . .
>
> . . . There have been reports that Dardik had run afoul of the USOC because of a conflict of interest with a company that manufactures cycling equipment . . .

This charge is fuzzy and unproven but, nonetheless, to my thinking, not completely far-fetched in view of Irv's demonstrable sales skills.

But the most compelling evidence of Irv's deceits comes from SRWE patients themselves. As I mentioned, I copied their names off the list Irv left in the cottage at "Irv's Camp," during my long wait for him to turn up to work with me. Some I already knew from the outset of Irv's program when, freshly brainwashed, I was enlisted as a de facto salesperson to give pep talks to the disgruntled and vice versa.

Gently and, above all, respectful of their privacy, I call several patients who confirm my misgivings about Irv: the wife (MS) of a theatrical director; the wife (MS) of an accountant; a physician (MS) who at one point threatened to report Irv to the AMA; an octogenarian and retired businessman (peripheral neuropathy); and a TV producer (chronic fatigue syndrome that was, in fact, a sleep disorder). All of them believe, as I do, that Irv is a cheat and a liar. They feel snookered by Irv and totally appalled by his greed and deceit.

Some, like the accountant's wife, whom I met personally, paid only sixty thousand dollars up front, plus excessive airfares for occasional visits from Irv's therapists. Irv himself showed up only once—to tell the man he would cure his wife and to collect his fees. The wife, using a cane when she began Irv's treatment, is now confined to a wheelchair.

Armed with all this information, I write to the New York and New Jersey medical boards:

December 22, 1992
New York State Department of Health
Empire State Plaza
Albany, NY 12214-0372

I am filing a complaint against Dr. Irving I. Dardik, a cardiovascular surgeon. I have severe, chronic multiple sclerosis and in June 1991 I was desperate. I had extremely limited mobility, I was losing the battle and learned I could lose all function within a few years. A friend sent me the enclosed *New York* magazine cover story on Dardik's wave theory of exercise and recovery and his alleged successes with MS victims. When I met this man, he enthusiastically told me he had the answer to MS, ALS, chronic fatigue syndrome and other chronic and fatal illnesses. He emphasized he was not talking about a remission; he could cure me. It would take a year and I would walk again. Unfortunately, I believed him.

When I was hooked, Dardik told me it would cost one hundred thousand dollars up-front because I was the equivalent of three patients, needed constant supervision and his hands-on treatment, and he would, therefore, not be able to take on new patients. When my family resisted, Dardik demanded fifty thousand dollars up-front and the remaining fifty thousand had to be paid within five months at a monthly rate of $8,333.33.

In addition, he made a profit from selling me and others a heart monitor and a useless computer program. He said it would enable him to predict high and low energy periods so he could do monthly exercise plans. This was never developed. He also asked me to answer an irrelevant questionnaire each day. At his request, I modified it for MS. He never used it. And I gave him a list of symptoms that was not used in his treatment plan.

Dardik's lack of concern became apparent immediately. He was so busy soliciting more business that he had no time for me and other clients who believed he was acting in good faith. I rarely saw him. He answered my phone calls immediately if I called with good news. It would take weeks to get a return call when there was a problem.

I believed him because I saw occasional improvements. I only recently learned the good moments I experienced were due, not to Dardik, but to 4-Aminopyridine, the experimental drug I'm taking. I continued treatment with Dardik until September 1992, because I made a commitment and wanted to make sure I gave him every chance to cure me.

Instead, his wave pendulum caused increased muscle weakness, repeated exacerbations, and I still have severe, chronic progressive MS. I'm now triplegic, I need a full-time aide to help me in and out of bed, to dress me, to bathe me, to use the toilet and clean my face and teeth. And, most egregious of all, his program imprisoned me and I paid a huge emotional price. I had to put my life on hold and give up my passion . . . my work.

Last year, I thought he was giving me back my life. Instead, he took a year I could not afford to lose. I have been told by three neurologists that my condition is significantly worse and I am now taking Imuran to, hopefully, stop or slow down the progression of my condition.

I want to emphasize this is not about the money. It's about good medicine, decency, honor and truth. It's about Dardik's negligence, deception, greed, about his taking advantage of the desperation of people who live with the prognosis of a question mark, about demanding an excessive amount of money up front for a worthless service he doesn't provide, and about ignoring his clients and their families when there's a problem. I've been waiting for over four months for Dardik to call me with an explanation for his failure to cure me or even stop the progression of my condition. To my knowledge, he has not cured any of his approximately forty clients. His therapists are decent people, but they can't do an adequate job because the program is critically flawed, they are not licensed physical therapists and they have to work, unsupervised, with three to five patients a day.

This man takes emotional and financial advantage of desperate people. I have received numerous calls from prospective Dardik clients who were quoted a higher price after showing interest in his treatment. He knew they would have to get a second mortgage and use their life savings to pay him a non-negotiable fifty to one hundred thousand dollars up front.

Dardik is negligent and dangerous. Before and during my treatment with his rigorous exercise program, he never examined me or asked for medical records. Although he was using exercise to quickly raise and lower my heart rate several times daily, he never did an

EKG. He never checked my blood pressure, asked for a blood test, checked pulmonary function (mine is only fifty percent), or tested my muscle strength and range of motion.

I have had several concussions from falls and when I fell and hit my head on a very hard tile floor, I called Dardik and told him I was in pain and had a severe headache. Dardik not only failed to examine me, he told me not to check with a neurologist.

When I complained about severe neck pain, he told me it was not serious. On my own initiative, I went to an orthopedic surgeon and learned the pain was caused by a herniated disc. Dardik never called the doctor or even requested a report. His lack of supervision caused the herniated disc, chronic and severe tendinitis in my right arm and shoulder and debilitating weakness in my arm and hand.

When I complained about overwhelming fatigue, muscle contractions and loss of upper body strength, Dardik assured me these symptoms would disappear. He said it was the result of a pendulum effect with the wave pattern. He said I would never get as bad as I was when I began treatment, and when the symptoms disappeared I would be better than ever. As soon as he got my heart rate up to 160, I would be able to walk. When I asked about doing range of motion and stretching for contraction and exercises for trunk balance and upper body strength, necessary for MS muscle memory, he said it was more important to get high heart rate numbers. His therapist got my heart rate up to 160. When it dropped to the low 40s, Dardik told me that was an expected response to his wave theory.

After four months of treatment in New York, I returned to my home in Orlando, with Dardik's approval and stated intention to hire a therapist to pay constant attention to my case. Well, that never materialized and neither did he except for one day. He sent a therapist to Orlando several times for a total of less than ten days. And he had the nerve to bill me for excessive airfares and demand I reimburse him for his therapist's phone calls to me.

I believe Dardik is guilty of medical incompetence, negligence and fraud. He needs to be stopped from endangering the health of chronically ill patients and from getting rich by cheating people who would pay any amount of money to regain their health.

I have enclosed copies of letters written to him. His one response quotes a few sentences from a letter my neurologist sent to me. He thought Dardik was a fake, but did not want to tell me because I was showing some improvement from a placebo effect.

He and the following neurologists can give you information on my condition and Dardik's treatment:

Dr. Steven Rosenberg

Dr. Herman Weinreb

Dr. Labe Scheinberg

As an investigative consumer reporter, daughter and sibling of judges and attorneys, I have always believed people should be held accountable for their actions and behavior.

Because of cheats like Irving Dardik, programs offered by reputable, decent and committed medical professionals don't get the support they deserve. All of us are potential victims of clever con men who can identify vulnerability. Irving Dardik is adept at this and needs to be stopped before he hurts or exploits more people.

If you need more information or have any questions, please call me or my mother, Judge Beatrice Burstein.

Thank you for your time and consideration.

Sincerely,

Ellen Burstein (MacFarlane)

The New Jersey board writes back that because of the volume of mail it will take many months just to read the complaint and decide if a further hearing is necessary. The New York office, however, responds immediately, scheduling an interview with me when I am next in New York.

Christmas 1992: Patricia and Jessica visit, and I blow up when they try to manage my life. After I tell them that I am having the steering wheel changed to make it light to the touch, they insist I give up driving: "What if your hands get weak?"

"What if they don't?" I reply. "Don't tell me what I can't do. Focus, instead, on what I can do. Stop treating me like a child!"

The van comes back with the light steering wheel, but within six months my hands become too weak to steer.

When my sisters return to New York, Patricia, a print journalist, decides to write a lengthy story proposal about Irv to send to several news organizations. Over the next six weeks, we talk by phone almost daily to craft the proposal. Patricia, whose hands work, puts it all together.

And out of her own curiosity, she calls one of Irv's patients mentioned in the *New York* magazine article. Reluctant though she is to be anything but entirely forthright as a journalist, nonetheless, in this circumstance, she can get a good handle on the story only if she disguises her identity.

On February 13, 1993, as Mary Murphy, who has MS, Patricia reaches a Nancy Kaehler, whom the *New York* magazine article says is "perhaps the most dramatic story." This Nancy Kaehler, a Philadelphia woman, tells Patricia that Irv doesn't like to work with MS patients and is now focusing on autistic children and cancer patients.

Says Kaehler: "He doesn't want to treat MS anymore because they're Type A personalities like this Orlando woman I met in New York. She's like the Ralph Nader of Orlando and, against Irv's orders, she returned there, went under the hot TV lights, took part in a marathon, and let her husband, whom she was divorcing, move back into her house."

Patricia and I don't know whether to laugh or cry; if I could run in a marathon, MS would not be a problem; if I could sit under hot TV lights, I would not have been approved for Social Security disability; and my divorce was final more than a year before I met Irv.

Kaehler also reports that she is now cured. To my knowledge, she had only minor problems with MS. I know this because soon after starting Irv's program, at a moment when I thought I might actually be getting worse, not better, Irv dispatched Nancy Kaehler to my sister Jessica's apartment, where I was then living, to deliver the standard spiel about the program. Kaehler refuses to say how much she paid Irv, only that she got a discount as one of his early patients and, further, because she does some computer work for him.

She counsels Patricia, alias Mary Murphy from Chicago: "If you write Irv a really heartfelt letter saying money is not a problem . . . you're willing to pay anything . . . then you could get lucky and he'll take you on even though you have MS." Kaehler tells Patricia that Irv is on his way down to the Caribbean—Aruba, she thinks—to get up a center.

It turns out that Irv is actually renting a villa in Barbados for his new cancer cure. For this reason, when several news organizations respond to our story suggestion, it has to be put on hold until Irv turns up again in the States. Further, we want to wait until the New York State Medical Board makes some determination, which may take a while since Irv, now in the Caribbean, also eludes them.

Patricia discovers another puff piece on Irv when she rings up a magazine to suggest a story on the agony a family goes through watching a daughter and sister with MS get deceived by Irv's promises and the total despair they feel later on.

An editor there, whom Patricia knows, says, "Oh, we already did that guy." Then, sighing, he adds, "It came from upstairs," meaning the owner. "This guy [Dardik] has a friend there." I know who this is because Irv blabbed about the man's son, an MS patient, whom he was visiting in another city, and how the mogul-father was going to invest in a center for Irv's program.

The article, written by a free-lancer from (excuse the pun) *Walking* magazine, claims in the subhead:

> Dr. Irv Dardik says his exercise therapy can cure chronic diseases. And he has the satisfied patients to prove it.

And in the article:

> Dardik has reversed the declining health of more than 40 patients with long-term disorders like multiple sclerosis, anorexia, bulimia . . .

Yet there is not a single quote from even one of over forty patients.

> There are doctors who respect his work, but even they are re-
> luctant to give credence to his claim of reversing nearly 90 per-
> cent of the cases of multiple sclerosis, etc., that he's treated . . .

Of course, there is not one single quote from any doctor saying, for example, he respects or will even pretend to attest to the veracity of his work.

In time, unfortunately, the owner of the magazine will also learn the truth about Irv, when his son, still somewhat ambulatory, gets worse. Unless, of course, his condition is only benign, he gets lucky and has no further exacerbations. I hope the latter will happen for him.

Assuredly, exercise doesn't hurt and may even help anyone who is well or just minimally ill. That, in part, is the beauty of Irv's scam: MS, being self-remitting, except with more advanced stages, can disappear on its own. Further, medicines can ameliorate symptoms such as those affecting bladder function. They are not relieved with Irv's SRWE program.

For the moment Irv has disappeared to Barbados in the Caribbean. By March, having decided to explore the possibility of a legal suit against him, we hire a private investigator, Alice Byrne, who actually has MS. A lovely, honorable, and pretty woman, whom Patricia met while doing a story on private investigators, Alice outwits Irv by a combination of enormous patience and her usual brilliance at subterfuge. It will take her many months to even reach Irv directly by phone because by now Irv knows I am on his trail.

Meanwhile, Irv makes a deal with the accountant whose wife has MS. He will repay their sixty-thousand-dollar fee in payments of ten thousand dollars every few months. In return, they must sign a legal paper, drawn up by Irv's lawyer, agreeing not to talk to anyone about Irv and his SRWE program. I am a little disappointed that this couple, so abused by Irv, capitulated to the gag order. But I can understand, for a young couple with children, how the return of sixty thousand dollars can make a vast difference.

In my case the one hundred thousand dollars my family paid would be a godsend because I now need round-the-clock care. I can't return to the job Irv instructed me to give up while he was supposedly curing me, and as a result, I cannot maintain the upkeep of my house anymore and will have to sell it. The cost of home care and the loss of income have caused unrelenting pressure and postponement of plans.

And, besides, how can I make plans when I don't know if I even have a future?

———

In March, I am in New York at our family home to see Labe, to meet with the medical board investigator about Irv, and to get a canine companion, a Labrador or a golden retriever from Canine Companions for Independence. These magical dogs learn some one hundred commands to help the disabled. Originally, I was supposed to get the canine companion in July 1991, but convinced Irv would cure me, I figured someone else should get my canine and I bowed out.

But, unfortunately, the sore throat I wake up with the morning I leave Orlando develops into the flu by evening. I am bedridden, need oxygen to breathe, and am able to move only my head. I think this is a preview of my life as a quadriplegic and I am terrified. I call Labe, who tells me the flu raises body temperature, causing a "pseudo exacerbation." He asks if I might be better off in a hospital. I say no because my mother has hired aides round-the-clock to take care of me.

I am finding that for every Irv there are many noble human beings in the health-care field. One of them, Dr. Mordecai Zucker, is a family practitioner who makes house calls for thirty-five dollars. In his early sixties, Dr. Zucker has alert and kind eyes. An Orthodox Jew, he models his life and work on Maimonides. In the neighborhoods around my family home, Dr. Zucker is known as "the angel." It is a well-deserved moniker.

Because I do not want to go into a hospital, which for me means the beginning of the end, paramedics come twice to the house to administer oxygen. Then an oxygen machine, which Dr. Zucker locates, is delivered and put next to my bed. I am terrified of what is happening to me and utterly devastated as well that, hard as I wish for my recovery in order to do the two-week canine companion training program, there is no possibility of this. Again, I have to cancel.

I am also too ill to travel to the city to talk with Tony Speciale, an investigator for the New York Board of Medical Examiners. So he comes to me instead, and barely able to get out of bed or speak, I manage to tell him my story about Irv. Ordinarily, interviews are held in their offices, where a doctor can also question me, but Tony, seeing my condition, understands that, clearly, there is no way I can get to the city.

During this time another Irv victim, with whom I talked back in December, sends me a copy of his letter to Irv:

March 15, 1993

Dear Irv:

I've waited as long as possible before writing you. It has been one year since you stopped taking or returning my phone calls. At that time, during one of our last conversations, you claimed you needed a few weeks to finish your paper, and temporarily had to lighten your work-load. I took you at your word, and decided to give you the slack you requested. I had been on the program for about a year, and in your opinion, required one more year in order to "lock in" my results. You had pledged to keep me on an additional year, or "for as long as needed." You pledged the same to . . .

Shortly after, you began to return fewer and fewer of my phone calls, and completely ceased sending "cycle assignments." In fact, as your "devotion" to keeping me on the program clearly diminished, and I was not getting cycles to do, I began to experience a serious sleep disorder (one that, even after a trip to a sleep clinic, I still struggle with). You took one of my phone calls and promised you could cure my sleeping disorder in one night, then said you'd be getting me back on the program very soon. I believe that was the last time I ever heard from you.

Irv, your total disengagement from me, especially at a time when I was experiencing problems, remains one of the most callous

and reckless acts I've encountered. It deeply saddens me to think
that your open displays of caring were hollow . . .

At first, I was going to chalk this up to just being had and move
on, but as the months went by I became angry at the idea that
when I had a problem, you, in spite of your pledge, dropped me
completely, showing a total disregard for the state of my health at
the time.

Sincerely,

Remarkably, I can move again after three weeks and at month's
end Patricia goes back with me to Orlando. Originally she plans to
stay a week but, after a conversation one evening, it becomes a
monthlong visit.

"Look what you've been through," Patricia says. "The most humiliating defeat, with the Irv scam, and yet you still go on. I think your
story should be told. Not just about him, albeit a major part, but your
courage. It would help other people."

Although I can no longer use my hands to write, my mind is unaf-
fected by MS. "You'll have to be my Number 2 pencil, Patricia.
Okay?"

I am really happy that she wants to do this, especially because she'll
have to dampen her ego in order to write with my voice.

She is at an impasse now with a second novel she has started to
write and confesses her desire to write something more substantive
than the celebrity biographies she has done more recently. The gene-
sis of my book, as it turns out, is the news story proposal Patricia and
I wrote.

It takes us a month to complete a first draft of the outline. When
Patricia leaves and I watch her back her rental car out of my driveway,
I think for an instant, *I'll never drive again, I'll never dance, I'll never walk
again. I have no future without my mobility.* But in the next moment, I
realize, *I'll get around on the printed page. This will be my future.*

Also, having a private investigator's license in Florida, plus investigative reporting credentials, I work with Alice Byrne, still on Irv's
case. So outraged is Alice, both as a private investigator and an MS

patient, she refuses to bill me for her services. No wonder she has been honored so often for her work, including heading up Child Find to locate missing children.

Indeed, she is one more angel antidote to Irv.

CHAPTER 17

I Don't Need Full-Time Care

Spring/Summer 1993

The flu really sets me back and I am very weak when I return to Orlando in April. Somehow, I can always sense when the MS is active and progressing, as it is now. I am losing strength again and my body shuts down several times a day. In addition, the nerves in my legs go into painful spasm; if contracting and releasing the muscles every few seconds to relax them doesn't work, I have to smoke marijuana—still another reason to legalize it for medical use. Labe stops the Imuran because it no longer works.

Although my mother keeps insisting that I hire live-in nursing aides, I am not ready to give up my privacy; it's bad enough that I need someone to bathe and dress me. Three days a week, Vicky gets me out of bed in the morning and stays with me all night. Another aide, Ann, is with me four days a week and, those nights, I am alone; I can still transfer independently from scooter to toilet and from scooter to bed.

In early May, I get great news: Canine Companions for Independence (CCI) has room for me in the July training class at the Farmingdale, Long Island, center.

I continue to see Bob five days a week for physical therapy and I am regaining some strength. And, before I go to CCI, I plan to spend a week in Los Angeles so Roy can work with me on my braces as well as readjust them.

I'm taking my aide, Ann, with me to LA on Sunday, June 13, 1993. On Saturday, I arrange to meet her at 7 A.M. the next morning at the airport. Vicky, who will drive me there, is coming to my house at 5 A.M. to get me up and dressed.

At 8:30 on Saturday evening, I experience my mother's worst nightmare: I have an accident when I'm alone. When I drive my scooter into a separate, cubicle-sized area of my bathroom to use the toilet, there are only a few feet of space to maneuver. As I get off the commode and transfer back to my chair, my legs lock. I slide off and go down on the tile: my legs are wedged and my right arm is hooked over an extension pole attached to one of the scooter's armrests. It hangs from the elbow down, which cuts off the circulation in my arm. I can't extricate it and the pain is excruciating. I can't reach the phone to call for help. My left arm is too short to reach the lever that turns the seat. Vicky won't be here until 5 A.M.—I am stuck for nine hours.

This is, by far, the worst night in all my nights with MS.

At 5 A.M., Vicky rescues me. My right arm, from the elbow to the fingertips, is very red and swollen. I scream with pain when she tries to move it and she calls an ambulance. Fortunately, X rays taken in the hospital show no broken bones and I am given prescriptions for Motrin and Valium. Vicky had paged Ann at the airport and she is at my house when we return from the hospital at 6:30 A.M. She panics and, against Vicky's instructions, calls my mother and tells her that I fell and had to go to the hospital. I am furious. It was so stupid and careless of her to wake up a seventy-seven-year-old woman, scare her, and give her incorrect information. When Ann insists she did the right thing and would do it again, I fire her.

Vicky calls her chiropractors, Sandra and Bill, very decent and caring people. For the next two days and nights, they put ice on my arm and shoulder. When the swelling goes down, they wrap my arm with charcoal and newspaper to warm it and soothe the pain. They save my arm.

However, I am now unable to stand up and transfer in and out of the wheelchair by myself because the meager use that I had of my right arm before this accident is gone, along with the rest of my independence. All along I figured that with a dog I could somehow circumvent the round-the-clock care. Nine hours on the bathroom floor changes my plans. I now need constant care.

———

True to form in my life with MS, there is good news. Patricia, who has just arrived in Orlando to help me, comes into my bedroom with a giant smile on her face: "A wonderful literary agent, Elaine Markson, is going to represent us!" A few days later, I talk by phone with Elaine and it is understood that because of my fall, Patricia will meet with her the following week in New York to discuss selling our book and to sign the agent contract. CCI training begins in three weeks, but talking to Elaine gives me such a lift that I decide to leave earlier with Patricia for New York to meet her. And now, when the rest of my family scolds about my fall, I can say, "Oh, it's just another chapter in the book."

Knowing I may have a new career as a writer makes it easier for me to, finally, leave my office at the TV station. All along Mike Schweitzer, my beloved general manager, has kept the office intact for me. It is now time to move on, and I feel fortunate that I can leave on my own terms. Patricia, R.C., and Vicky help me clean up my office and pack. It takes under two hours—I'm saving only files I will need for my book. I give my furniture to Vicky's daughter, a college student.

This is another ending, another beginning.

———

Before leaving I talk to Ruth Gale, a real estate agent, about selling my house by the latest, February 1, 1994, due date for my book and also my forty-ninth birthday. Once in New York, I almost lose my new agent. When we meet near her office in a handicapped-accessible restaurant, which has a very long staircase, my scooter loses control and Elaine is nearly pinned to the wall as I crash into the table. She survives without injury. She is very witty and bright. I like her immensely.

My twin, my Number 2 pencil, signs the contract for both of us. Softly, and perceptively, Elaine says my book is, above all, about love. And she is right. It is all about L-O-V-E, as I began to understand after my fall three years ago on the cement and later on from my family.

Jessica goes with me to see Dr. Weinreb and a pain specialist about my arm and she is fuming when the doctors ask, "You were on the floor for nine hours all on your own? No one was there?"

"Ellen," Jessica says after one doctor gives her this strange look, "the way you tell this story of your fall makes it look like no one cares about you. It's as if you have this family, they must be thinking, who just forgot about you and don't know or care how long you lay on the ground." Jessica is right. But somehow her telling me this makes me laugh. I promise to change my story.

The doctors want me to postpone getting my canine companion so I can undergo therapy, but I cannot cancel again. So we compromise on injections to relieve the pain, as well as physical therapy instructions for the nurse's aide who will be with me during the program.

On July 12, 1993, I begin the two-week training program for my canine companion. Again, more angels appear in my life. They are Ellen and Ann, the instructors, and the beautiful golden retriever that will eventually become my best buddy.

This is such a pure charity. Though the actual cost of breeding, raising, and training each dog is over ten thousand dollars, I and the other lucky people who get one pay only a twenty-five-dollar application fee and one hundred dollars for necessary supplies. Because it costs so much to train these working canines, there are too few of them and a year and a half wait. For the most part, CCI breeds border collies for the hearing-impaired and Labradors and golden retrievers to help the disabled and autistic children. In the latter circumstance, through loving interaction with their dogs, these children, locked inside their own worlds, begin to connect a little better with other people.

There are seven, including me, in the class: two parents of autistic children; a U.S. marshal, paralyzed by a cervical spine injury; a chemistry student paralyzed from a motorcycle accident; a teenager with cerebral palsy; and a paramedic with MS.

It is a grueling two weeks, appropriately called "boot camp." After eight hours of classes and training with the dogs, we have to study at night for daily tests. The dogs are much better trained than we and we have to learn how to get their attention; to get them to obey a hundred commands, which include opening doors, turning lights on and off, and retrieving fallen objects. We also go on field trips to shopping malls, restaurants, and movies so the dogs can practice taking money out of our hands, giving it to a cashier, and then bringing back receipts and merchandise.

The first two days, we work with several dogs. But I have an immediate rapport with a golden retriever called Imus. The dogs are named by the people who raise or give ten thousand dollars for their training, in this case, the New York radio personality Don Imus. This is the perfect dog for me: laid-back, loving, loyal, strong, and very smart. The instructors try different canine/people combinations for two days and then decide which dog goes to which person. I am ecstatic when they bring Imus to me.

Since I don't want to be asked later on, at every stop, if he's named after a radio host, I change his name to Butter, which matches his light golden color. My mother, sisters, and brothers come to my graduation. I speak for my class:

> In learning to communicate with our dogs, we learned a lot about ourselves. If I could stand up, I would give our instructors, Ellen and Ann, and everyone in the Canine Companions for Independence program a standing ovation.

197

I explain to my family that Butter is not a pet but a service dog and for the next few weeks no one is allowed to pat him or even make eye contact because we must bond. Remarkably, everyone, including my mother, who appears to be smitten as well with Butter, shows restraint. But I need to work with him without distractions so I return to Orlando after a few days at the family house.

During the two weeks at CCI, I had a wonderful and truly smart and competent aide, Inge Cassagnau. About fifty, she is a handsome and sturdy woman, from what was, sorrowfully, once Yugoslavia. If I could only find someone like her in Orlando.

Before I return to Orlando with Butter, there is great news on two fronts. One is that my book has been sold to a very respected editor, Lisa Drew, a vice president of Macmillan Publishing Company with her own imprint. When Patricia and I meet her, we are greatly impressed and like her immediately. Lisa has a crisp mind and a kind heart. Over the course of writing the book, she will be the most civilized book editor Patricia says she ever encountered. Not only does Lisa respond with comments within a day or two of receiving pages, but she actually edits! I feel really blessed to have such an honorable, talented, and caring editor.

The other good tidings: Alice Byrne, private investigator, has finally nailed Irv to a consultation at his New Jersey farm. He is reluctant to take on any MS patients until Alice tells him that money is not a problem. She is scheduled to see him on a Saturday in late July.

Throughout, her timing has been impeccable; she has been patient so Irv wouldn't think she was acting on my behalf. Alice has also been enormously inventive, convincing Irv a rich uncle died and she has to attend to his empire, which, of course, she inherited. Alice first gets a call to show up in Barbados to see Irv. She bows out using the excuse of an alleged sprained ankle. Meanwhile, she gets Irv on tape trying to lure her down to Barbados even though heat, especially summer in the tropics, exacerbates MS.

Irv's new theory is that the closer patients get to the equator, the better the cure rate. It is true there is little incidence of MS among people who grew up in warm climates as opposed to the northeastern

United States, an MS cluster area. However, Irv's latest discovery has one major fallacy: if someone grew up elsewhere, say the Northeast, like Alice and me, relocating to an area close to the equator is absolutely useless.

Alice has all of this and more on tape. Some of the best dialogue:

IRV: And it gets to be such an interesting—you hear these guys, hear [*unintelligible*] they're having a ball. Can you imagine having a ball with leukemia?

ALICE: Yeah [*laughs*].

IRV: And feeling like you're on top of the world.

ALICE: Yeah.

IRV: Can you imagine? Listen, when you come down here you'll see a guy named David . . .

ALICE: I just talked to him briefly. He answered the phone, at least.

IRV: David, David is senior vice president for . . . Yeah, now here is a guy with kidney cancer with metastasis in his abdomen, on his skin, and all that. When we saw him he was a mess. He was depressed, he was dying. He was skin and bones. He was really falling away from mental and physical depression. He was dying.

ALICE: Yeah.

IRV: It was awful. His life, at sixty years old, was gone.

ALICE: Yeah.

IRV: Well, he just turned sixty last week. We celebrated his birthday.

ALICE: Oh, how neat.

IRV: Well, let me tell you something.

ALICE: Yeah.

IRV: The guy took up golf.

ALICE: Yeah?

IRV: He now is—he plays—I don't know if you know anything about golf—

ALICE: A little, but—

IRV: He shot a forty-two for nine holes—

ALICE: Well, that's pretty good . . . It sounds like Club Med.

IRV: Oh, it is . . . astounding.

ALICE: That's very good. That's very good.

IRV: His best, two weeks ago, three weeks ago, was forty-nine.

ALICE: Yeah.

IRV: His coordination, where he was . . . You talk about your coordination.

ALICE: Yeah.

IRV: You have to see this guy. He was—he couldn't do anything physically. He couldn't even figure out how to put one foot in front of the other.

ALICE: Well, I—

IRV: And now suddenly this guy is playing golf. And you'll talk to him, you'll see what I'm talking about.

ALICE: Right.

IRV: It's—it's masterful what happens with coordinating the physiology to make this thing work right.

Typically, at some point, Irv puts another leukemia patient, a doctor, on the phone to tell Alice how brilliant Irv and his program are. Five minutes later, after an ode to Irv by this man, Irv gets back on the phone and says this patient was dying and, what's more, his doctors back home are amazed. However, in a later tape, this same patient says he has not told his doctors and, instead, wants to walk in and surprise them.

At some point Alice and Irv discuss finances. Originally, Irv tells her fifty to sixty thousand dollars but now that he knows her financial picture, her so-called heiress role, it will be one hundred thousand dollars for his hands-on treatment:

IRV: Look, here's—here's the scoop in terms of these finances, which I really didn't want to go over with you on the phone. I mentioned to you it was fifty to sixty thousand dollars when I, you know [unintelligible], depending on, you know, whatever the—what—

There are two possibilities. One is, when I have a therapist working with someone, who comes in now and into their homes

200

and works with them and does things by phone, and—so we have a bunch of patients who we work with on that scale.

On the other side of the coin are the people that I work with directly that we've involved ourselves with here. They're only a handful, in which I'm actually organizing every bit of this.

And there are only three or four people here that I've been able to do that with. And it's more expensive, because of—and you'll see. I mean, if you meet the people, you'll see. You know, you can come here and decide if you want to do it the other way around. That's fine.

The people that I work with here directly, and—personally supervising every aspect of this, it costs one hundred thousand dollars for the year. For the other side, for the—for the—fifty to sixty thousand dollars is when we work on a more limited . . . You know, I—I'll tell you, one of the people here I charge absolutely nothing. Zero, essentially, because she's just a fantastic person. Her husband went bankrupt and I just said come on down, and I'll work with you and work with the others so that they were able to pick up some of her expenses. She's a woman with breast cancer, and she's just a phenomenal person—

When, eventually, Irv returns to New Jersey and Alice goes for a scheduled consultation, he pulls out the records of his many patients—so much for confidentiality: he labels me a troublemaker and pot smoker, which, he argues, is the reason why his treatment didn't work and I'm not walking; he complains about the magazine mogul's son being difficult. And, forgetting what he said about MS, Barbados, and the equator, Irv now claims he prefers to stay in Boston and Florida.

Irv's wife, Alison, parading around the swimming pool and sun porch of the house during Irv's four-hour manic recitation about the program, chimes in and says there is a fifteen-hundred-dollar consultation fee that she will waive. She later faxes Alice a contract, asking for a nonrefundable fee of one hundred thousand dollars for a year—fifty thousand dollars upon signing.

They spell Alice Byrne's name wrong—Alice Burns—not surprising because, after several earlier phone conversations with Alice, Irv asks, nonchalantly, "Oh, by the way, are you ambulatory or in a wheelchair?" Nor does he ever ask her medical history, leaving this to his secretary to do in a cursory fashion by phone. Nor does he request reports or contact Alice's regular neurologist, whose name she gave the secretary.

Above all, on tape, when Alice asks Irv if his treatment is a cure, he says, simply, "One hundred percent, no ifs, ands, or buts."

On the basis of Alice's brilliant work, my lawyer-brother Judd files a Federal RICO (racketeering) civil suit against Irv on August 2, 1993, in United States District Court, Eastern Division of New York.

Judd's opening legal salvos:

Plaintiffs ELLEN BURSTEIN MACFARLANE and BEATRICE S. BURSTEIN, by their attorney, Judd Burstein, P.C., complaining of the defendant herein, allege as follows:

NATURE OF THE ACTION

1. This is an action seeking damages for a violation of the RICO statute (18 U.S.C. 1961 et seq.), as well as for a common law fraud. From at least March of 1991 through the present, Dr. Irving I. Dardik ("Dardik") has intentionally and reprehensibly schemed to defraud multiple victims through the use of the mails and wire communications. Preying upon the desperation of those suffering from severe and chronic illnesses, as well as their families, Dardik promises a "cure" in exchange for excessive amounts of money in advance. The "cure," however, does not exist and, in fact, the purported treatment is nonexistent and worthless. In essence, Irving Dardik is nothing more than a modern-day snake oil salesman.

2.   Plaintiff Ellen Burstein MacFarlane ("MacFarlane"), who suffers from severe, chronic Multiple Sclerosis, is one of Dardik's victims. In June of 1991, Dardik, knowing it to be untrue and expecting MacFarlane to rely on his advice, promised that he could "cure" her disease through his unconventional program of "making waves" through

radical exercise and recovery. In connection with the commencement of this program, Dardik induced plaintiff Beatrice S. Burstein ("Burstein"), MacFarlane's mother, to turn over $100,000 to him by a variety of intentionally false representations, including the representation that he would pay constant attention to her daughter throughout the recovery period of one full year.

3.   Thereafter, and contrary to defendant's false promises that he would "cure" MacFarlane and, specifically, that he would have her walking within the year, she is now a triplegic who requires a full-time aide to accomplish the simplest of daily activities. Moreover, after receiving monies in advance, defendant virtually disappeared.

4.   As a direct result of defendant's fraud, plaintiffs have been damaged in the following ways. First, in order to participate in defendant's program, MacFarlane was forced to give up gainful full-time employment and, because she is now permanently disabled, she may never be able to return to work again. Second, MacFarlane was required to purchase extensive exercise equipment, a heart monitor and computer programs, all of which have turned out to be useless in treating her disease. Third, Burstein was induced to turn over substantial sums of money to defendant to fund what amounted to be a nonexistent treatment program for her daughter's Multiple Sclerosis.

5.   Moreover, as detailed below, Dardik's fraudulent conduct vis-à-vis plaintiffs is part of a much broader scheme to defraud others suffering from severe and chronic illnesses through virtually identical false representations. These multiple mail and wire fraud schemes, all related by the virtually identical nature of the false representations, constitute a pattern of racketeering activity.

Irv's response to the complaint is not surprising—he denies the allegations. At the date of this writing, the case is still pending. So, too, is the New York State Medical Board investigation. And the New Jersey Board of Medical Examiners has finally followed suit. The next time I see Irv will be, I hope, at a medical board hearing or in a courtroom. And, this time, he'll be the one who needs help.

As I used to close my stories on the air, "I'll let you know."

In August I return to Orlando and start interviewing nurse's aides. Sadly, Vicky is recovering from an illness and is no longer strong enough to look after me. However, she keeps a key to my house in case of an emergency and we speak frequently by phone.

It is difficult enough to hire one aide in a hurry but I have to find three of them, write a book, and work with my canine companion, Butter. So far I have not had terrific experiences with aides.

First, there was Maggie, who, after working for me for two months, decided she wanted to quit. However, she neglected to tell me this. Instead, she failed to show up the next morning and I was unable to get out of bed until I could reach Vicky five hours later to come over and rescue me.

Next was Ann, who had the poor judgment to call and frighten my mother after my nine-hour bathroom accident. And she has yet to pay back the twelve-hundred-dollar advance I gave her for the Los Angeles trip.

It is an enormously difficult job to find people who are willing to put their patients first and to perform intimate tasks like bathing, changing diapers, and inserting suppositories. With many patients, aides sit by their beds just waiting for them to make a movement or request. But in my case they must constantly be attentive and in motion because I am so active and energetic. And it may take ten minutes for them just to get my leg in the right position so that I can balance myself when sitting.

Patricia, who arrives within days of my return to Orlando, is insufferably grumpy. She wakes up every morning in a rage about having to be in Orlando, which she doesn't like, and about Churchill, Beijing, and Butter sharing the same space with her, because she's uncomfortable with dogs. Above all, she is in a panic about beginning the book, which is due six months from now.

But in her calm moments, when she's not quoting Gertrude Stein on Oakland—"there is no there there"—about Orlando, she is enormously caring and protective. She is also highly perceptive about people and I will ask for her opinion before I hire someone.

Ultimately, out of the three nurse's aides, I make one bad choice, Glenda, a twenty-two-year-old woman. I didn't listen to Patricia when she told me that she was uncomfortable with this woman's personality. I hired Glenda, in part, for her large size, helpful in lifting me, and her seemingly alert and pleasant disposition. Also, she appeared to be trustworthy.

Five months later I will learn that Patricia's instinct about her was correct. This is a woman whose personal problems distract her and whose mood swings are too extreme for this kind of work.

I lucked out, though, when I found Nancy Beaudoin, thirty-four, a woman who won't give up until I'm physically comfortable and whose clean, pure laugh reminds me of the sound of chimes. Since working for me she has felt encouraged to return to school to further her education. I am very proud of her achievements and growth as a human being.

Similarly, my other aide, Bonita Stamper, twenty-nine, is extraordinary. I think she is the most patient person I have ever met. She is certainly one of the most decent too.

Both Nancy and Bonita have become integral parts of my life and I consider them family.

Were I still on television, I would investigate how the "Maggies and Glendas" of the health-care profession get or keep their licenses. I think it is critical that there be some safeguards for people like me whose safety is in the hands of home (nurse's) aides. We are extremely vulnerable because these aides get involved in the most important details of our lives and, feeling no family obligation or loyalty to us, can just walk away with our secrets.

Were it not for both the watchfulness of my family and my reputation in Orlando, the "Maggies and Glendas" might have been able to do a lot of financial and emotional damage.

During this time I also have to give up Churchill and Beijing. Aside from a territorial conflict with Butter, it is impossible for the aides to take care of me plus three dogs. Trouble is, Churchill, twelve years old and blind, and Beijing, ten, are too old to be adopted. So, if I can't find another home for them I'll have no choice but to have them put to sleep.

This time Brian really comes through for me. He takes them to Houston, Texas, where, until recently, he worked as a news manager of a TV station. Sadly, Churchill became so incapacitated that Brian had him put to sleep. We will both miss this wonderful dog.

Brian and I speak frequently and to my great pleasure, he has regained his confidence, sense of humor, and gentle nature. Now the news director for a TV station in Lafayette, Louisiana, Brian is back doing what he's good at and what engages him. Once again, we are terrific friends.

We will always love each other and I know he will always be there if I need him.

CHAPTER 18

My Family Speaks

January 1994

I am blessed. My main angels: my family. My kind, wise, gentle, and generous mother, Judge Beatrice Burstein; my brilliant, thoughtful, funny, creative, talented, and loving brothers and sisters, Karen, Patricia, Jessica, Johnny, and Judd.

Though I do not believe in using or being used by MS, I must admit that it can be a convenient excuse for my siblings when they want to get out of a meeting: "Sorry, but Ellen doesn't feel good. I have to stay with her." But I forgive them. Even I sometimes use the MS: "I would love to straighten up the room, but I have MS."

The MS is not a solitary loss. It is a family sorrow. And, unfortunately, this is often overlooked by others. It would be much easier if I gave up and did not resist the MS, because then my mother and siblings would not have to continually adjust their lives in order to make mine more comfortable.

I know that their discomfort increases along with my physical deterioration and it is horribly painful for them. They feel guilty about avoiding me. And I feel guilty about disrupting their lives.

Yet, I never feel unwanted or unloved. And, although they see my disability when we're together, they don't think of me as disabled.

It takes so much love and courage on their part to allow for all the changes in my condition, the never-ending unpredictability of my MS. So I have asked my mother and my siblings to write about their feelings. I want them to know that I wish I could make it easier for them. I want them to know I understand. I want them to know that I love and respect each of them, with all my heart.

My Mother, Beatrice Burstein

Writing about what has happened to my daughter Ellen is extremely painful. And I am sad that I am not a demonstrative person as my late husband was. So frequently, I feel like hugging Ellen and telling her how sorry I am that this terrible illness is consuming her, but I am unable to express myself.

Instead, some of the time, I find myself being so angry about the MS that I make inappropriate remarks that hurt her feelings. For example, for months and months, I urged Ellen to hire round-the-clock nurses. I told her that, if she chose to remain living in Orlando, the only way I could get a night's sleep was if I knew someone was looking after her all the time. Then, in June 1993, on the eve of a trip to Los Angeles for her braces and therapy, she fell and injured herself. When I found out that same morning, I was sobbing, thinking about her lying there, helpless for nine hours, on the floor.

I was also furious with her and when, finally, Ellen came home to Lawrence, I could not restrain myself from scolding her. Knowing she was still in pain, I looked at her and said, "You can't complain—you did this to yourself. What can I do about this? You promised me there was a nurse's aide all the time. Why did you conceal this from me?"

My anger is really anger at the disease itself. It reminds me of visiting Ellen just prior to her divorce and objecting to Brian's irritated voice when my daughter dropped something. "Why do you talk to Ellen in that tone of voice?" I asked him, and he answered, "You don't understand, Judge, I love Ellen, but I hate the disease."

I visit Ellen in Orlando as infrequently as possible now because it is just too painful for me to see her. Previously we all took turns going almost weekly. When I call her on the phone, she always tells me, "I'm okay," and I never know what that means. She is so busy trying to protect me from the worry and sadness I feel anyway.

There have been other times when I got angry at her. Visiting her, just about the time she started using a scooter (motorized wheelchair), I went with her to her TV station. She insisted on using a walker and it took a half hour for her to reach the newsroom.

It was excruciating to watch her struggle, bent over the walker, and trying to drag, push, her legs to move. Afterward, I said in an irritated voice, "Why didn't you use your scooter?"

"I don't want to look disabled."

"Ellen," I said before I could stop myself, "you're being unrealistic. You look more disabled, struggling so with the walker, this way."

In my thirty years as a judge I could resolve most any problem for someone else. But with Ellen's illness there are no answers to her agony or mine and there seems to be no solution.

My own life has been extraordinary. I had a wonderful husband and all six of my children are honorable, decent, and productive. Outside of my husband's death, Ellen's illness is the very worst thing that has happened.

I feel so sorry for Ellen and, in truth, myself as well. Though mandated to retire three years ago I am still working as a judicial hearing officer for the Appellate Division in the courthouse. I enjoy remaining productive and I do a good job. But one of the reasons I continue to work is mental—to distract myself from the agony of what the MS has done to my daughter.

Though, at seventy-eight, I have the time and the financial resources to do most anything I like, such as traveling, I am unwilling to indulge myself because I want to ensure that Ellen will always be protected. Sometimes I think it is probably a good thing that my husband died before Ellen got multiple sclerosis because he would have pressured her to come back home or flown to Orlando fifteen times a month, and despite his loving motivation, diminished her feeling of independence. I'm not sure either of them would have survived the other's strong will.

It is time now, Ellen feels, for her to move back to the family home, where I have lived for forty-four years. At my age I worry that if I should become disabled myself, the house will have to be sold because none of my children want or can afford the financial burden of its upkeep.

Although I know that, if I became ill, all my children would be concerned about their sister, I do not want any of them to become caretakers and I have told them this. Ellen agrees. Yet I'm not so sure Patricia does.

As it stands, having lived on my own for over a decade since my husband's death, I have become accustomed to my privacy. So Ellen's arrival will require some adjustments on my part. One of them: biting my tongue when I get angry at the MS.

From her, in return, I want only that she express her feelings. Even as a child she always held her emotions and thoughts back. I am so proud of my daughter Ellen—her nobility and bravery as a human being. But as I have said to her, when a particularly difficult situation arises, "Ellen, you can cry. You are entitled to cry."

I've often said that, if I had my life to do over again, I would have been a different and better mother. That I can't change. But, in a way, Ellen is giving me a second chance.

This time I shall seize it—with many hugs for my beloved daughter Ellen.

Patricia Burstein

Walking to school in the spring, under the dogwoods and cherry blossoms, my twin sister, Ellen, and I believed that our lives would be lived so easily. That nothing bad would ever happen to us.

It did, three decades later. At age forty-one, Ellen was diagnosed with multiple sclerosis. It is eight years later and she is confined to an electric wheelchair and robbed of the ability to bathe, dress, comb her hair, or even scratch her head on her own.

Until MS arrived in her life, we had pretty much lucked out. We were children of considerable privilege, growing up with four other siblings in a rambling house filled with books and classical music, and our parents gave us every opportunity to grow and to stretch our talents. There were travel and study abroad; private schools; Christmas holidays in the Caribbean; college and graduate school; and the freedom to choose a profession, not just a job. If there was pressure to succeed, to be special, there was also room to fall down.

From our parents we also learned that pleasure could be taken as much from ideas and words as from people. Always, they tried to shield us from unpleasantness and inconvenience. However, they did not think it was necessary to prepare us for unwanted surprises.

But for me there was an omen, a suggestion even then, that illness could interrupt our lives. When we stayed overnight with Nanny, our adored maternal grandmother, we knew that there lived below her apartment this woman, always dressed in black, including her shoes, and scrunched in a wheelchair. She was paralyzed from polio.

Whenever the elevator stopped at her floor, my knees buckled and my heart pounded and I hid in the folds of my Nanny's lamb's-wool coat or cotton frock, depending on the season. I prayed that this woman would not be parked outside, waiting to get in the elevator with us. I was terrified of this woman in the wheelchair.

Of course, it seemed unimaginable then that someone I love, my twin sister, Ellen, would also end up one day in a wheelchair.

Another fear, perhaps less instructive, that accompanied my childhood was of large dogs. They frightened me, almost as much as the woman in the wheelchair. I depended on Ellen to chase them away. In return, I would carry her schoolbooks, including a rather large loose-leaf notebook, along with mine. Though I could barely see over the pile of books grazing my nose, all that mattered was that my twin kept her word as my protector.

Now, all these years later, I wish that I could be her protector and chase the MS from her life.

As a print journalist for two decades, I had abandoned this, my true labor of love, to write books. Somehow I found myself off-track. My twin, meanwhile, was flourishing in her career, having located her calling as a television investigative consumer journalist, with a grand measure of success and respect from the community where she worked. All the while, I thought of her as the plodder and myself as the poet.

How wrong I was. In writing Ellen's book with her, I have been constantly amazed by her extraordinary intelligence, wit, clarity of thought, and devotion to words. In a way I have gotten to know my twin all over again and in a new and refreshing way.

Working together has yielded still another bonus: spending a great deal of time with her. While at times other family members may step away from the MS, I find it has brought me closer to my twin.

Many nights, during the writing of this book, Ellen and I labored, either by phone or at each other's side, until three o'clock in the morning. At some point, suddenly aware of the lateness of the hour, I'd instruct: "Go to bed right now . . . You can finish the chapter tomorrow . . . And did you eat proper meals today?"

Before I could even finish lecturing, Ellen would interrupt, protesting, "You're not my mother . . . I'm not a baby . . . And when you keep bothering me about what I should do, all you succeed in doing is disrupting my concentration."

And if the truth be known, it is Ellen who is the parental figure with me instead of the reverse. Her wisdom tempers my occasionally dreamy, foolish, and impossibly romantic and unruly self. She also trims letters I compose which are unsuitably long and cleans up my grammar.

It would seem that, as the bigger and stronger twin, the athlete, I should have led the way. But then, as now, that has not been the order of things in our lives. And when the MS attacked her body, I continued, even as an adult, to hide from life's unpleasantries and inconveniences, which she, on the other hand, managed to take in stride.

She stood up to the MS, fighting it, step by step, while I grappled with grandiose plans—nothing less would do—that only served to paralyze me and set me up for failure even before I had begun.

It baffles me when other family members mention how "wonderful" I am with Ellen. I do not see it this way—not at all. Quite to the contrary, the amount of time Ellen and I spend together has only to do with the pleasure of her company, never guilt or duty.

Probably it is a truism that usually when a family member becomes ill there is one sibling who may be a bit more attentive than others. That person, in more recent times, has been me. In part, it is because as a writer, my schedule is more flexible than that of, say, a lawyer.

But I feel, over these last eight years, that all of my siblings, particularly Jessica, have been equally present. In any event, one of the lessons I learned from Ellen's illness is to respect others' emotional boundaries: people, sisters and brothers included, can only do what they can at a particular moment. And I'm no angel all the time, raging as I sometimes do against the MS.

I do worry about our mother, who is the cohesive, unifying force in this family. She is seventy-eight, and with her husband, our father, dead more than ten years, the heartache she feels about Ellen's illness is a lot to absorb. An eminently practical and wise woman, always, she makes the right decisions.

Ellen's illness holds several lessons for me. The incremental moves, the small victories, allow her to find her footing and even after the MS stalked her, she continues to move beyond what, at first, she considered just a minor inconvenience.

Her MS has also made it possible for me to begin again, this time taking baby, instead of giant, steps. I have no choice. To help her means adjusting my expectations—just as she does daily with the unpredictability of MS—to remain strong and focused. Not even the pain of divorce or continuing loss of body function can unhinge my twin. Watching her helps me to find my bearings.

Often when I am swimming, I fantasize trading places with her: two weeks out of each month I sit in the scooter and she swims; the other two I'm back in the pool and out of the scooter. I dare not tell her this.

Were she still able to put pen to paper, she would write this book herself. More likely, she would type it on her laptop. As someone who always moves forward, in this case keeping pace with the latest technology, she is something of a computer wizard. Here again, I lag behind, still grappling with a primitive word processor.

Nonetheless, she has asked me to be her scribe. However, the voice, original and distinct, belongs to her alone. Once again, she resolves still another of my quandaries, which is, am I writing because I have something to say or because I just want to say something?

I am proud to share the experience of writing this book with Ellen. In her words, I am her Number 2 pencil.

Karen Burstein

My sister Ellen is never far from my mind, but days can pass, even weeks, before I speak with her. The truth is I hate that she is sick and that she will not get better and that there is nothing I can do to make her well. So, it's easier to push her into a corner of my consciousness—a knot of awareness, a touchstone, available when I need to reassure myself that I care, but far enough off in that corner that I can get on with my own life.

Of course, sometimes, the pain moves to the center of my awareness. When we are together, there is no escaping it. Even as we talk seriously about her plans, laugh at the idiocies of mutual acquaintances, tell tales of my courtroom, I must cut her food, break medicine into a cup of liquid and bend the straw for her to sip it through, watch her, with glacial slowness, pick up an item, type a word, shift, my hands moving her legs, to find a comfortable position on her seat. It is unforgivable, I know, to want to go away from there. But it is true. For such heartbreak, the only anodyne is distance.

I don't remember her well as a child, which is strange. I felt, as the firstborn, a strong responsibility for most of my brothers and sisters, almost as if I were their parent. Somehow, though, Ellen escaped the reach of my concern. I have pictures in my mind of a chubby, pretty, needy little girl, but not someone who relied on me, as her siblings did; not someone who shared her secrets with me, showed me her treasures.

Indeed, my strongest memories of Ellen, except one, are associated with illness. Those memories have the quality of photos—bright, immediate, time-limited but immensely evocative. I flip through them now and see:

I am standing in an airport, Kennedy I think, waiting for a plane to arrive, to deliver Ellen to me and my mother. She is recovering from a sudden and terrible operation—an infected cyst in her womb that burst and flooded her in her own blood. They caught it just in time, but only because she, schooled as a medical reporter, knew to keep forcing her gynecologist to believe the pain she was suffering was real. Where she went after she left the plane, how much time I spent with her—all this is a mist.

But I learned, somewhere in that period, about the black cat she had nursed all through a terrible night and that, until he died (or was given away), was as attached to her as an infant to a mother.

Again, I am traveling with my brother John in my parents' limousine to a mental hospital in Connecticut. To my astonishment, Ellen has asked me to accompany him so we can all participate in a family therapy session. I know that John and Ellen are close, but until we meet in a small room with the therapist, I don't understand why I have been chosen by Ellen to appear. She says that she always considered me a parent substitute: someone who would care about her and take care of her.

Initially, I swell with pride, and then such self-regarding feelings disappear in the raw pain and love and need of the session. I promise myself never to forget what happened; now I don't know what was said, but I can still capture, fleetingly, how happily exposed and unabashedly open I felt to both Johnny and Ellen and how grateful, after the tears, I was that they were my family.

Despite Ellen's evident clarity and sanity, the hospital administration resisted releasing her that day. Ellen was convinced that this position flowed not so much from a concern for her psychic integrity as from an interest in milking the last drop from her rich insurance policy. Whatever the institution's motives, it took me a good two hours of stamping my feet, pulling legal rank, threatening suit, and arguing, by analogy, what I imagined was Connecticut law, to spring her.

But spring her I did and John, Ellen, and I rode out of the place laughing heroes to ourselves, proud of our unwillingness to yield to "superior" medical knowledge, full of Burstein hubris. I see us giggling in the car, confident that things would only get better, that the worst had passed.

For a while, things were good. Ellen moved to Florida; she became a star. I visited her in their first home. For some unremembered reason, Brian was not around that weekend. Instead, we hung out together, eating Alice B. Toklas brownies and leading half of the visitors to Disney World on a merry chase. (At one point, at the head of the line, Ellen and I entered a theater, moved to the end, and then shuffled out, followed by a line of one hundred; when we were back on the sidewalk, it suddenly occurred to everyone that we had missed the show, but it was a great walk.)

That weekend, the only time I spent alone with Ellen while she was a fit adult, taught me interesting things. I was impressed by her discipline; she ran every morning. I was moved by the seriousness of her commitment to her work; she took phone calls from disgruntled consumers at the house. But I noticed how irritable, how volatile, how impatient she was, if her plans were frustrated, if her listener didn't grasp her meaning immediately, if her companion wanted to pursue a course she had not marked out.

My sister Ellen taught me, without meaning to, a great deal about myself, for all of these are my traits too and I might never have seen them so starkly, never have been willing to try and change them, had I not been the object of behavior that I came to realize was typical of my own. I left Florida happy with my new closeness to Ellen, relieved to be out of her demanding presence, and committed to monitoring the way I acted toward others.

Several years passed. My father died; I changed jobs; I entered a committed relationship. Throughout, Ellen was on the periphery, friend, sister, colleague. And then she began falling; not climbing stairs well; feeling unaccountably weak. Finally, someone suggested MS and she came back from Florida to consult the expert in the field, Labe Scheinberg at Einstein. I brought her up there or met her there each time.

It's an interesting facility, bright, with a warm waiting room and quiet places for examination. But it's a hospital and there are always patients in chairs and walkers waiting to be seen or just leaving after consultations. A place where disease lingers, where problems get identified, not solved.

I know, because I was doing the same thing Ellen always did, entering the place in opposition: "I am not like the others; I can walk down the hall faster and straighter than anybody else who has MS; my symptoms are passing phenomena; I am here only by a horrible accident; I am going to wake up and discover this was all a mistake."

Her yearning, mine, the family's, for proof that it hadn't really happened to her was contagious. Labe said she would dance on his grave. Her numbers never really seemed to worsen; then, one day, she was fine. MS can burn out; if you live long enough, you can outrun it. And here was Ellen, strong in limb, without Babinski's, her bladder in control, her balance restored. She had beaten the disease. I see us in my car, laughing, confident, Bursteins triumphant again. Maybe ordinary people have to suffer, but not my golden family, not my special sister Ellen.

We were wrong, all of us, wrong: my father, who taught us that Bursteins are exempt from the terrible accidents of fate that afflict others; and Labe, who saw Ellen's special quality and the way she responded to the medicine he prescribed and insisted she would keep walking; and the rest of us, my mother and brothers and sisters, who believed in the magic of being a Burstein.

It is later. I am in Florida and Ellen is very frightened. Labe has told her she is weeks away from a wheelchair. She has deteriorated dramatically; the weakest and shakiest I have ever seen her. I reassure her anyway; with her will, we'll find a way. And, dammit, I believe it or I want to believe it so much that it becomes real for me.

Now, it isn't the aura of the family that will save her; it is her bright, passionate, burning conviction that she will not be disabled, that one day she will run again. If we can buy some time, science will cure this disease.

My pictures get shuffled here; time blurs in my mind; I don't know when, in this sequence, I saw Ellen at home in Orlando, playing me the tape of Brian's betrayal—Ellen torn between rage at him and pride in herself for figuring out how to wire the recorder so he wouldn't know she was on to him.

Unlike Patricia, who has still not figured out how to set the station buttons on a car radio, Ellen is a technophile. She loves tinkering with electronic equipment; she sees quickly the way things work and how to manipulate them. Configuring a computer and running are, I think, special triumphs for her because they are skills so at odds with what one would have expected from the unathletic, chubby, unconfident little girl she was.

Ellen became a woman of sure competence; she could order her world, fix a leaking faucet, get a recalcitrant printer to deliver clean copy, shape her own body neatly and tightly. And the MS makes a mockery of all this achievement, laughs in its face. It brooks no refusal. It gives no quarter. It takes away the dexterity of fingers, the limberness of legs, the control of muscles. It doesn't give a damn how disciplined or smart or focused you are; and it's evilly fickle.

Sometimes, it pretends that it isn't serious. Ellen can seem, suddenly, fine, stronger, more mobile; and then she crashes and the fact is, she doesn't get to choose either state. But we don't really come to know this for sure until after the hospital, after the chemotherapy.

Jessica and I go almost every day and spend hours with her, talking or sitting quietly or lifting her up to pee into a chair/chamber pot or accompanying her to the toilet so she can smoke some dope before the ice-cold fluid is pumped into her veins, the toxic medicine which will kill her cells to clean them of the illness . . . if it works . . . if it just works. She is tiny and pale in the hospital, but alert and loving and unself-consciously vulnerable.

There, for those days, when hope still exists that the pain and the ice and the killing serum will stop the relentless slide of her body into paralysis, Jessica and I and Ellen joke and gossip and cheer each other on. And I, who grew up modest, even in my sisters' presence, change Ellen's diaper, blot up the urine that misses the pot, see her naked without embarrassment or discomfort, only sometimes with sadness at how difficult natural functions are for her.

At last, we are all of us in the car, going home, stopping to buy Depend at a grocery in the Bronx, convincing each other that now that the regimen is finished, this weakness will eventually leave, that Ellen will be restored, if not to full mobility, at least to steady strength and health, pushing out of our minds what more objective eyes would see. That she is worse, not better; that she is weaker than ever before, her arms and hands more flaccid, her legs shrinking in mass.

It is not so surprising then that we all, in different ways, buy into Irv's program, are willing to suspend our disbelief, are prepared to invest real hope and a lot of money in his promise of a cure.

I see Ellen on the stationary bike in Jessica's apartment, doing her cycles, capturing the data on the pulse monitor she wears around her wrist, pushing herself relentlessly, arguing plausibly that you have to hit bottom first before the waves can carry you up. Yes, yes, it's true; she doesn't seem to be any better, but her enthusiasm is infectious, it buoys us, it helps us deny the evidence of our senses.

We believe in justice, we Bursteins; we believe that good triumphs, that hard work is rewarded, that you get what you pay for. My mom is paying one hundred thousand dollars; Jessica is paying in loss of privacy; Ellen is paying in sweat and pain. How can it not come out all right; how can such virtue not be rewarded? Irv told Ellen she would run again; I remember her face glowing with her faith in that promise. Hope is a compelling seduction. And its betrayal, bitter beyond words.

I am angry at Irv, but angrier still at myself and at this disease. And if I am truthful, at Ellen, for being sick, for interrupting the certain flow of my life, for making me know that something can't be fixed for all the will and money and wishing in the world. And my anger becomes a justification for shutting down, for absenting myself.

219

If I am not around Ellen, I don't have to see what I don't want to see. We are emotionally febrile people, we Bursteins, and our feverishness scares us, so we have become very good at shutting down. We are masters of denial and avoidance. Ellen says that as she has gotten sicker, she sees everyone but Patricia pedaling fast in the opposite direction. And she is right.

Ellen's voice on the phone is strong and healthy, her mind sharp and clear; to hear her only, to converse with her from a distance, is to forget she is ill. To see her, particularly if some time has passed, is to be hit in the stomach with the truth.

And yet, the truth is a complicated thing. Sleeping unmoving in her bed, carefully positioned under the covers, she looks so tiny and helpless. Watching her struggle with a straw, I am overcome by sorrow and pity, and then she utters a sharp command or laughs an unrestrained laugh, her eyes bright with impatience or pleasure, and she is so alive you know that sickness is a mere contingency: that the MS hasn't touched her essence, except to anneal it into shining steel.

There are moments when I completely forget she is ill and I am mad at her because she is so unreasonably demanding—of me, of her nursing aide, of anyone who happens to walk into the room the minute, and it is the minute, she needs something done. There are times I think she is unbearably self-absorbed and careless of others. Only on reflection do I see the value of such an ego, such an unapologetic confidence that attention must be paid, for Ellen's continued capacity to overcome the disease's blandishments.

She has never yielded gracefully to its constraints. She stopped walking, she sat on a scooter, she allowed people to feed and bathe and exercise her begrudgingly, after a mighty struggle. T. S. Eliot said that we are undefeated only because we go on trying. In this struggle between Ellen and MS, I watch with loving awe as she keeps on trying to wrestle the evil thing to the mat.

After all the false hopes and high promises, after all the disappointment and disillusion, after all of this, when the match is finally over, I am sure of one thing. The MS may be the technical victor, but it will be Ellen who has truly won.

Judd Burstein

My reaction to my sister Ellen's illness is one of my great disappointments in life. In many ways, I have not risen to the occasion. I visit and speak with her perhaps less than any other family member. I have spent a great deal of time trying to understand why I have not acted as compassionately as I would have hoped. I think I understand the reasons.

Prior to her illness, Ellen and I were more alike than any of our other siblings. Both of us had distanced ourselves as young adults from the family, choosing instead to find emotional sustenance elsewhere. Although we always had a wonderful time speaking to each other, I do not believe that we communicated, either by telephone or in person, more than four or five times a year.

I think that I continued to keep my distance from Ellen because of my inability to face up to the full scope of her tragedy. In my own mind, a change in the nature of our relationship would require acknowledging the depth of her illness. Thus, in some perverse way, I have sought to view her as more healthy by not radically changing how we interact.

In the back of my mind, I have clung to the view, perhaps false, that if Ellen really needs me on an emotional level, she will call me. I have always felt a deep responsibility toward my brother and sisters such that I would be there for Ellen if she communicated such a need. Our mutual silence on the issue gave me an easy out. I am relieved that my brother and sisters, as well as my mother, watch over Ellen in her day-to-day life.

I was grappling with all of these issues when the problems with Irving I. Dardik arose. A lawsuit against Dr. Dardik has permitted me to show my sister that I do care about her and that I can devote time to her. I am disappointed in myself with this arrangement. But this is the best I can do for her at this time.

John Burstein

I met my older sister Ellen when I was twelve years old. Sure, I had seen her around for years—at family functions, at meals, passing in the hall, etc. But I never really knew her. She was just one of the bunch. Besides, everyone in my family was so busy guarding him/herself from attack that keeping people at a safe distance was considered good survival strategy.

One night that began to change. I wandered up to Ellen and Patricia's (the twins') room. I don't remember why. Ellen was sick, perhaps with the flu. The room was darkened and she was in bed. For some reason, perhaps the feelings of loneliness, vulnerability, or boredom that sometimes accompany illness, Ellen started a conversation with me. A very different kind of conversation from any we had ever had.

Instead of asking about my day at school, she wanted to know how I "felt about my life." "What was it like growing up a boy?" "Wasn't Daddy scary?" We talked for a couple of hours about our inner worlds and discovered that we were "kindred spirits."

I believe there is a defining moment for most people when they suddenly wake up and become aware of their own existence. It is when the realization dawns that we are all separate, and hold a strange, miraculous, and frightening lifetime in our hands.

Somehow, by chance or grace, my "waking up" coincided with Ellen's interest in me. We became real friends and allies. We began to protect and defend each other from my father's attacks at the dinner table. We achieved the unimaginable: we learned to trust each other.

As a boy entering adolescence, I was deeply insecure and full of questions and conflicts. Ellen was there to help me figure things out—to support and encourage any emerging feelings of self-confidence. I looked up to Ellen for guidance and I gave her some things she had not experienced very much—love, respect, and complete acceptance.

I remember how sad I was when she left for college. I remember how excited I was when she invited me for a weekend visit. I can still clearly picture packing new dungarees for the trip and feeling so grown-up and jazzy. I was off to college to "hang out" with Ellen.

As the years passed we shared a developing belief in spirituality: a faith that there was something going on beneath the surface. I remember one evening talking to my family about looking up at the nighttime sky and thinking about "the language of the stars." I should have kept my mouth shut. Everyone else laughed and made fun. But not Ellen. She knew what I was talking about.

Over the next twenty years, Ellen moved all over the country and I would visit her a couple of times a year. We had a bond, warm and caring. We weren't like the archetypal college friends who could see each other once every five years and pick up on the same conversation as if no time had gone by. Our relationship was different. We were not peers. She was always my older sister.

We were family. And we were family by choice, not by accident. We were open with each other. I remember when Ellen got a job in New York at Eyewitness News. I felt incredibly jealous. I couldn't help myself. As children we had learned that parental love and acceptance were given as payment for achievement. But as this love and acceptance were always in short supply, if someone got a big dose, everyone else would be left out. There wasn't enough to go around.

We felt proud of each other around outsiders, but within the family another sibling's achievements would usually make me feel diminished. But Ellen and I could talk about this. I could say, "Your success makes me feel like a failure." And she would understand, accept, and appreciate the honesty. And so I was able to untie some of my internal knots.

As I said, Ellen and I did not have a peer relationship. She was my older sister and therefore she protected me from her fall into deep depression. When she attempted suicide, I was shocked. I never knew that life had become so painful for her. Yet, when it came to visiting her at the hospital, my sister Karen and I were the only ones she wanted to see. I was scared, but I believed she would pull through. And, of course, she did. But I always wondered what seeds of self-destruction were sown at that time.

I was with Ellen right before she discovered she had MS. Along with my mother, we were vacationing together in Rio. This was another example of our closeness. We enjoyed being together and were out for a walk around the hotel. Ellen kept stumbling. Every few hundred yards, she'd trip slightly. She told me that it was "lazy ankle," a condition brought on from her regimen of running. We joked about it.

After we returned to the States, Ellen's condition deteriorated and she discovered it was MS. I had no idea what that meant. When I visited, we still worked out together in her exercise room. Early each morning she'd go off to work and we'd go out for dinner in the evenings. She appeared healthy and vital. MS seemed to be only a minor inconvenience and I never believed or could conceive that there would be a downward spiral.

My family was not supposed to get sick like this. We were too special, too strong. And Ellen and I believed in spirituality. "As you think, so you are."

I was convinced that Ellen could meditate her way out of this illness. But that approach didn't work. Then I thought she'd found a way to exercise her way out. That didn't work. Or she'd chemotherapy her way out, or find a Bulgarian cure. But she kept sliding.

Somewhere along the line, I began to slide myself. Not into illness, but away from Ellen and into retreat. I look back over the last two years and see that during that period I have visited less often and had less communication with Ellen than at any other time since I was twelve.

I'm not really sure why. The easy answer is to say that it is simply too painful to experience this illness up close. But I'm not sure that is the whole of it. I know that MS scares the hell out of me. It points out life's unfairness, highlights the arbitrary nature of existence. It forces me to confront my own vulnerability and, without question, my mortality. I hate this illness. And since I have not made my peace with it, I cannot spend much time with my sister.

If I ignore it, maybe it will go away. And on some bizarre level, I believe that if I don't use this time "meaningfully," I'm not admitting Ellen is sick. Therefore, I'm protecting her. I don't see her because she doesn't really need me. She doesn't really need me because she's not really sick.

I no longer know how to share my problems and concerns. They all seem so petty. How can I talk about all the things I'm doing, my marriage and professional successes, when her life has become so confined. What a sad predicament. Once again, I need my sister's help. But this time it's to help me work through my resistance to her disease.

I began my true relationship with Ellen when she was sick in bed. It opened up a new chapter in my development as a human being. Once again Ellen is ill, and I must find the courage to take this opportunity to grow. I love my sister—I love her very much!

My Sister Ellen

Someone forgot to tell us
That life could be unkind.
We traveled the road
That was paved with gold
And we never lagged behind.

We kept the pace
Of the winner's race
And we danced to the gifted's tune.
We hopscotched over life's little cracks
And we gathered our rosebuds soon.

We dashed so fast
And we jumped so high
And if we had a fall
We bounced right up
Because we knew
That it was nothing,
Nothing at all.

But one day en route to the finish line,
Running the lap
To the cheers
Of the years,
A headwind blew down
And we looked around
To find . . .
Someone forgot to tell us
That life could be unkind.

—Jessica Burstein

Washington, D.C., 1973.
Photo by Jessica Burstein

Lawrence, New York, 1993.
Photo by Jessica Burstein

CHAPTER 19

Carpe Diem: Seize the Day

February 1, 1994

How do I go on with so many losses? I need assistance to move my right hand and arm and both legs, to brush my teeth, wash my face, bathe, feed, and dress myself. Because of "drop foot," I, again, wear AFO braces on both feet along with shoulder, elbow, and wrist braces that give support and relieve pain. I have replaced my three-wheel scooter and its two-hand steering control with an electric wheelchair and joystick. I am also unable to transfer my body independently, open an envelope, or even sign my name. Often, I use a mouthstick to type on my computer.

Yet, much to my surprise, I am not ready to surrender, nor will I go down without a fight. Though there can be no restitution, ever, for what the MS has done to my body, I don't waste energy crying about the "what ifs." Instead, I am learning how to live with "what is." I never think "Why me?" but, rather, "Why *not* me?" And I intend to focus on trying to make a difference in the lives of others; the homeless, the disabled, anyone who is vulnerable.

In August 1993, Butter, my aide Bonita Stamper, and I arrive at the Home Depot parking lot. A young boy stares with awe as the lift carries me and my electric wheelchair out of my van and down to the ground.

"Cool, man," he says, apparently impressed with my "designer disability" wheelchair. I have customized it with black and gold polka-dot seat covers, gold automobile trim, blackout tape, and carpet on the chair and I have painted the silver screws with gold nail polish.

Bonita takes Butter for a walk on the grass, and as I wait, the little boy sidles up to my chair to take a closer look.

"I wish I had one of these," he says shyly.

"I'll race you," I challenge.

"I'm fast," he says, crouching down.

"Let's just see. On your mark, get set, go!" At the sound of the chair's horn, we take off.

It's neck and neck, but he wins. I congratulate him, say good-bye, and warn him that I'll be back for a rematch. Butter, Bonita, and I then head for the entrance to Home Depot. Once inside, Butter retrieves a roll of electrical tape from a high shelf and brings it to me.

From behind me: "Look, Mommy, a doggie."

"Don't touch, Erica."

I turn and see a small child who looks about six years old. Butter wags his tail. I smile. "Hi, Erica, say hello to Butter. He wants to shake your hand and give you a kiss."

She giggles with delight as Butter licks her face. "How come he's in the store?" she asks.

"He helps me."

"Why do you need help?"

"My legs and arms don't work like yours."

"Oh." Erica turns to her mother. "Can we go with them?"

She is disappointed when her mother says no.

We say good-bye. Butter gives Erica another kiss.

"That was wonderful!" I say to Bonita as we leave the store. "Kids are usually scared when they see someone in a wheelchair." But my track competitor in the parking lot and Erica did not see my disability. They only saw a lady with a "doggie" and a fancy chair.

Bonita laughs. "Erica would have gone home with us."

I think these children could teach adults about looking at a person, not at a disability.

———

Almost eight years ago, multiple sclerosis crept into my life and forced me to change how I lived it. I never looked at a sunset, I just knew it got dark; now I am nourished by the vibrant colors as they fade to black. Like a child, I am seeing things for the first time. I've learned to hear, not just listen; to see, not just look. And, above all, I've rediscovered my family: they've taught me how to give and how to love; my mother and my brothers and sisters enrich my life.

I wish MS had never happened, but I would not give it up if it meant reverting back to the kind of person I was. The truly disabled are the thoughtless people who cannot see beyond a cane, a walker, or a wheelchair: the employers who refuse to hire; the shopkeepers who won't access their stores; the agencies unwilling to provide services; the families and people who neglect and discard. All of them make it impossible for people like me, less able-bodied though no less able-minded, to lead productive lives.

It has been a difficult and painful journey through MS and I could not have done it without the great faith that there is some reason for all of this. For every bad moment, there are three good ones. And, always, I have hope.

MS is only what has happened to my body; it will never define me or control what I believe. In or out of a wheelchair, I stand proud of who I am and what I do with my life. I am, finally, whole and at home inside myself. I am enlarged, never diminished, by my condition.

One night seven years ago, a voice woke me from sleep: "Don't worry, Ellen, you'll be just fine." I now know this was not a message about my future physical condition. It was about me.

And, yes, I am just fine!

Index

INDEX